NO ONE LEFT

WHY THE WORLD NEEDS MORE CHILDREN

Paul Morland

FORUM

FORUM

This paperback edition first published 2025
First published in Great Britain by Forum, an imprint of Swift Press 2024

1 3 5 7 9 8 6 4 2

Copyright © Paul Morland 2024

The right of Paul Morland to be identified as the Author of this Work has been
asserted in accordance with the Copyright, Designs and Patents Act 1988.

Typeset by Tetragon, London

Printed and bound in Great Britain by CPI Group (UK) Ltd, Croydon CRO 4YY

A CIP catalogue record for this book is available from the British Library

ISBN: 9781800754126
eISBN: 9781800754119

To Claire, my co-pro-natalist
And to our grandchildren, Leo and Hallel
May they be the first of many

CONTENTS

CONTENT

PART ONE

EXTINCTIONS AND EXCEPTIONS

M AKING the case for having children has never been more urgent.

Making the case for having children has never been more difficult.

Urgent – because of the impending collapse of populations in community after community, country after country, continent after continent. Overall world population continues to grow, but at an ever-slower pace. Population decline, already stalking an increasing number of the world's nations, is now clearly in sight at a global level.

Difficult – because of changing preferences and because of a rising tide of attitudes that are combining to persuade more and more people to have fewer and fewer children, or none at all, and are making it harder to challenge anti-natalism in a growing swathe of society. Once it was material progress that drove falling birth rates. Now, in much of the world, it is ideals and lifestyle inconsistent with family formation and populations replacing themselves generation by generation.

The purpose of this book is to draw attention to the problem, understand its ideological and material causes and suggest what we might do about it if we want people to thrive or even to continue to exist. Nothing is more important to the future of humanity.

I

THE INFERTILE CRESCENT – THE LOOMING DEMOGRAPHIC ARMAGEDDON

A spectre is haunting Europe. It is also haunting East Asia and much of North America, and before long it will be haunting most of the world. It is the spectre of depopulation. For decades this has been nibbling at the peripheries, the remote rural regions and smaller rust belt towns, and we have largely ignored it. These are not places where opinion-formers like journalists, academics or politicians tend to live, or to which they pay much attention. But now its consequences are hitting the headlines. And this is just the beginning.

We are seeing the birth pangs of a new epoch, but it's an epoch without birth pangs. You can trace a path in a great arc from the Straits of Gibraltar at one end of the Eurasian land mass to the Straits of Johor at the other, and travel only through countries facing the prospect of population decline in a vast infertile crescent. Included are countries with Protestant, Catholic, Muslim and Buddhist majorities, rich countries and poor countries, democracies and autocracies. For some of these places the phenomenon is new, for others it is decades old. Almost irrespective of social, economic or political characteristics, these are states and nations where population decline and its consequences are being baked into the future right now.

'Russia running out of "single-use" soldiers'; 'UK running low on fuel, truck drivers'; 'Staffing shortage continues to disrupt Amsterdam Schiphol'; 'China's factories are wrestling with labour shortages'.[1] The headlines cover different countries and economic sectors. Each of these labour shortfalls has its own local and specific characteristics and causes: the Kremlin's initial reluctance to announce a draft, the UK's withdrawal from the EU, poor handling of the Covid disruption by Dutch (and many other) airports, a growing Chinese preference for white-collar jobs over labour on the factory floor. But underlying these stories and many others is a much bigger story, a reality that is spreading across the globe like wildfire: we are running out of people. The cracks are just beginning to show.

Whatever the particular conditions of a time and place, whatever the other causal factors, these shortages of people would not be occurring if, 20 to 30 years ago in the countries concerned, people had been having two to three children instead of one to two. The UK government's 2023 budget, for example, focused on pension reforms to get early retirees back into the labour force, no doubt a laudable and possibly achievable goal in its own right. But the demographic imperative would not be there at all if the population of people in their early twenties still outstripped those in their late sixties by 1.6 million, as it did in the mid-1980s. Today, there are just 170,000 more people in their early twenties than in their late sixties.[2] The net inflow into the workforce is therefore down nearly 90 per cent.

The robots and other technological devices have been promised, but if we want our dripping tap fixed, our supermarket shelves filled or our elderly parents cared for, machines are not about to charge over the horizon to save us. We still need people to do things, just as we always have. We are already short of them, and it is only going to get worse.

This seems a bold claim when the world's population has just reached 8 billion, its highest ever level, and is continuing to grow. But scratch beneath the surface and a very different picture emerges. Yes, the number of people on the planet is still growing, but the rate of growth has halved since the 1970s and is continuing to fall. And while the overall number of people is gently peaking – the upward slope ever flatter, the impending zenith ever closer – humanity is rapidly ageing. More and more of the global rise in human numbers is about delaying death, while less and less is about the creation of new life. Reduced mortality is eclipsing new life as the driver of population growth, but death can only be delayed for so long.

Taking a global view obscures much more dramatic occurrences at national and local levels. It is nationally and locally that people in Asia, Europe and North – and, eventually, South – America will lack everything from plumbers to surgeons. As their countryside empties out and their suburbs are abandoned, as their schools shut and their villages rot, any compensatory population growth in Burundi is of little comfort and less use. Immigration is a possibility, but its effects can at best only be partial and temporary, as we shall see. And not every country with a population shortfall is rich enough to attract or fully willing to accept large-scale immigration from those ever-rarer parts of the world where birth rates remain high.

In a small number of countries, the total population is already falling. In a growing number of countries, the working-age population is in decline, while those reaching retirement age are ballooning in number. There are fewer and fewer young people ready to enter the workforce, now that much of the world has experienced half a century of 'sub-replacement fertility', which is what happens when couples have on average fewer than 2.1 children. In the UK, for example, we have not had above-replacement fertility since the early 1970s. In Russia, you would have to go back to the 1960s. Despite technological innovation, our economies continue to be addicted to endless inflows of fresh workers. When these inflows seize up, so too do the petrol supplies and the airport luggage trolleys.

The great global population implosion will have major geostrategic implications, just as the great population explosion had from the nineteenth century. First-off-the-blocks Britain was able to dominate vast tracts of the globe by settling them with its burgeoning number of people, transforming places from San Francisco to Sydney. The same will be true on the way down: some places will see their populations crash faster than others, and this will shape the history of the next century.

The impact will also be felt at the most intimate level. I have recently been paying regular visits to an old-age home in London. It is almost entirely dependent on a staff of recently arrived immigrants. For those who cannot afford their services, or for countries unable to attract them, there will be nobody there to care for the elderly. And the entire economic system will creak and perhaps collapse as those too old to work grow in number while those of working age shrink. Great powers will wane. The elderly will die unattended and alone. And everything between the geopolitical and the personal will change, and not for the better.

STAGES OF DECLINE

To maintain a stable population, the fertility rate, which is the number of children born during the lifetime of the average woman, needs to be slightly above two. Previously that number was much higher, because as many as a third of children died before the age of one, and perhaps two-thirds of people died before completing their own fertile years. But in most of the world, where a vanishingly small proportion of babies now die before the age of one, and a very small number of people die before the age of 50, slightly more than two children per woman is enough to keep things on a long-term even keel.[3]

Population decline comes in three stages. First, the number of births per woman falls below replacement level. If there has been earlier population growth, there will be plenty of young women giving birth and relatively few old people dying, so population growth will continue, for a time. This is known as 'demographic momentum'. Second, the large cohort of low child-bearers starts to die, and their own, less numerous off-spring bear few children, so deaths start outstripping births.[4] 'Natural decline' sets in, although in countries that are attractive to migrants, immigration can temporarily stave off an absolute reduction in the population's size. In the final, third stage, the absolute number of people declines despite ongoing inflows of migrants.

For countries that cannot or will not attract migrants, stage three is reached directly from stage one. Britain is moving from the first of these stages to the second: the margin of births over deaths remains positive but it is very small, and only immigration prevents labour shortages being even worse than they are. Germany is moving from the second to the third stage, with migration no longer high enough to offset the natural fall in population as deaths increasingly outstrip births. Russia and Japan have leaped directly from the first to the third stage, as has China, where the latest data show the population falling by 850,000 a year.[5] Throughout these stages, the population ages and the number of those economically active declines.

SELF-REINFORCEMENT

'Demographic momentum' may help delay the fall in population, potentially long after the point where fertility rates have gone sub-replacement. But if fertility rates ever rise back above replacement level, the reverse effect can be felt. We might call it 'demographic drag'. A rise in fertility rates among the current generation of people of childbearing age is the only way to reverse the decline in numbers, but it takes a long time before it actually does so. This is because the cohort of potential childbearers is simply too small and the cohort of elderly dying is simply too large. Deaths will continue outstripping births for a time. In Japan, for example, the number of women aged 15 to 45 is down by more than a quarter from its 1990 level, so even if every woman were having the same number of children as were women at that time, a quarter fewer would be born. By the end of this century the UN estimates that there will be around half the number of Japanese women of childbearing age as there are now, so again, even if their fertility rate per woman remained unchanged, the numbers born will have halved. This is how a population can, and in many cases probably will, go into a demographic tailspin.[6]

There are other ways in which low fertility rates can reinforce themselves. One, for example, is through the expectation and experience of family size.[7] When people have small or no families, conditions for those with children are likely to become more difficult. Less thought will be given to accommodating the young in urban design or product design, making it harder to get about with buggies, or find suitably sized accommodation or cars. A second way is that societies with small family sizes set the expectations for future generations. Those from large families have historically been ready to adjust themselves to having small families, but not vice versa, creating a downward ratchet in family sizes.

A third way happens when care for ageing parents features significantly in the lives of adult offspring, and there is less time to devote to child-rearing by those who are single children with no siblings to share the burden with. In China, where many of those caring for today's elderly are only-children married to only-children with similar responsibilities themselves, the idea of having to raise their own children while simultaneously supporting their increasingly frail parents seems daunting. 'We are struggling to take care of our mum, but at least we have siblings that we can share this burden with,' says one middle-aged Chinese woman. 'A couple with an only child will need to take care of old parents from both sides, which is four old persons. Can you imagine what kind of burden our generation will become to our children?'[8]

THE HISTORICAL CONTEXT

While the public may be somewhat aware of declining birth rates, they tend to think that somewhere else, for good or ill, people are still having lots of children. There is nothing new in this. In the nineteenth century, casting anxious eyes over the Rhine, the French feared that the Teutonic woman was endlessly fertile. But the generation of Mutti Merkel (despite the name, she and many of her contemporaries are not *Muttis*) has proved them wrong. In fact, low German fertility rates are now a century old. While it was once the case that the Germans in turn feared the endlessly fecund Slavs, in reality, Olga bore a large family for only a few decades longer into the twentieth century than Helga did. And as for the supposedly child-oriented Italian *mamma* surrounded by a large brood, that's a myth now well past its sell-by date: Italian families have long been among Europe's smallest.

We all know about the Chinese one-child policy, but now it is becoming clear that even when the Communist Party allows people to have more children, the Chinese don't want them. The same is true of their ethnic Chinese sisters and brothers in places where they were never subject to the Communist Party's population controls (in Taiwan and Malaysia, for example) and of other peoples in East Asia, from Korea to Thailand. Their family sizes fell sharply in the latter part of the twentieth century even without the coercion prevailing in the People's Republic of China.

A century or more ago, conscious of Asia's demographic weight, people of European origin (then the fastest-growing people on earth and politically preponderant) spoke nervously of the 'Yellow Peril'. More recently, people in the developed world fretted about the loss of jobs to a China replete with vast numbers of cheap labourers. But having got used to hundreds of millions of Chinese workers meeting their every manufacturing need, Europeans and North Americans might soon come to miss their abundance and how cheap their labour was. For the first time ever, China has ceased to be the world's most populous country. And although that title has now passed to India, all is not well south of the Himalayas either. It is a surprise to many that the average woman in Kolkata has but a single child. West Bengal as a whole has a fertility rate below the UK's. The trend is catching on across India. In fact, the only difference between the world's two demographic giants, China and India, is time, with India just a few decades behind China in plunging into demographic deficit. As India enters into the first phase of population decline (fertility below replacement level), China is entering the third (absolute population decline). Both countries are too poor to attract mass immigration, and too big for immigration to make much difference in any case.

FIRST GREYING, THEN DISAPPEARING

The future looks demographically bleak across much of the world. This is showing up most visibly in the data on ageing. Within Europe, Italy is a particularly stark case. In 1950 there were about 17 under-tens for every one person aged over 80. Today the two groups are matched roughly one-to-one. But it is not just in relatively rich, developed countries like Italy that this is the case. It is also true of countries on the path to prosperity, which have made great strides but still have a long way to go. If Italy typifies Europe, Thailand typifies developing

Asia. In 1950 there were more than 70 under-tens for every one person over 80. Today the ratio has slumped to three or four to one. Within a generation the over-eighties will outnumber the under-tens.[9]

The ageing of a population comes with some advantages: there's generally less crime and a lower likelihood of going to war. But it also means a shrinking workforce and a declining tax base at the same time as there are rising demands on the state for pensions and healthcare. Those aged in their late eighties or older require six or seven times as much health spending as those in the prime of their lives. When the UK's NHS was established, there were 2–300,000 such elderly people in the country. Today there are well over 1.5 million, and by the century's end there will be getting on for 6 million.[10] Small wonder that ever-higher spending on healthcare yields little by way of perceived improvements for individuals.

This is why countries like Japan and Italy, with among the world's oldest populations, have the highest government debt-to-GDP ratios in the developed world.[11] The consequences of social, economic and fiscal stress are clear. The sluggish growth of the Japanese economy since its workforce peaked more than three decades ago is very evident, with not just a relative decline of the economy as a whole, but also on a per capita basis. As the country grows older, its people get relatively poorer. GDP per head in Japan was just 18 per cent below that of the US in 1990; today it is almost 40 per cent lower.[12]

This is not just social change. It is complete social transformation. It has implications for everything, from crime and punishment, to war and peace, to boom and bust. Given the general shift to low fertility that seems to be almost universal, we could see rapid population decline to a quarter of the current 8 billion, or below, over the next three centuries or so. In the longer view of history, the period in which humans exceeded 2 billion people could come to be seen as a relatively brief and, in retrospect, peculiar spike.[13]

According to the best estimates, Japan will have lost more than 40 per cent of its population by the end of the current century, as may China. The losses thereafter may slow, but they may continue until they leave behind ever-shrinking, isolated communities, incapable of sustaining strong nations, and less and less capable of functioning. In South Korea, at current fertility rates, each cohort is about 40 per cent of the size of the last. Run that forward for just three generations and you lose nearly 90 per cent of your people. That's what will happen, although a bit more slowly, if fertility rates in countries as different as Malaysia and Macedonia remain at their current levels for a few more generations.

In many places like China, stabilising the current fertility rate as opposed to letting it continue to fall will only make population decline gentler. For a perpetual decline not to set in, fertility rates will need to rise significantly, back to above replacement level, which would be more or less unprecedented. The self-induced population decline we are seeing today has never happened before in human history. It is time to start worrying about it. It is high time to start talking about it.

BUT SHOULD THE POPULATION GROW FOREVER?

It might be argued that the world was a fine place with 1 billion (around 1800), 2 billion (in the 1920s) or 4 billion people (in the 1970s). Why would it matter if it went back to those kinds of levels? What would be an ideal population? Need we go on growing our numbers forever?

Of course, the world in 1800, 1920 and even 1970 was a much poorer place than it is now. A much larger share of the population lived in penury and hunger. That might seem paradoxical: after all, there was all that extra space and all those extra resources per head when there were fewer people. But as the nineteenth-century American economist Henry George pointed out, both chickenhawks and people like chickens, but the more chickenhawks, the fewer chickens there will be, while the more people there are, the more chickens. Human inventiveness is the key to additional resources, whether it involves smarter ways to produce food or more efficient forms of capturing sunlight and wind for cheap energy. A world with more people, and specifically more educated people, which is what we are achieving, is a richer world. If plenty of space and potential resources per head were all that was required for human prosperity, our ancestors would have been immensely materially richer than us, rather than immensely poorer. Singapore, with a hundred times greater density of population, would be much poorer instead of hugely richer than Burkina Faso. And Bangladesh, with a population that has more than doubled since it gained independence more than 50 years ago, would have grown much poorer instead of much richer.

I made this point following a recent interview during which I espoused pro-natalist views and suggested that the world would face a crisis of too few people, not too many. One of the comments on the video asked whether I had ever travelled on the trains in India, the implication being that with so many people, India's transport system was bound to be a chaotic. I answered that I had, and that doing so in the 2010s was an infinitely better experience than in the 1980s, even though India had doubled its population in the intervening years. India has better rail transport (and much better air transport) now its population is 1.5 billion than when it was 750 million. Higher population density and prosperity have made investing in infrastructure much more viable. Go back to 1800, when India had around a tenth of its current population, and of course at that point it had no railways and no air travel at all. The assumption that things get worse as the world gets more crowded simply does not hold up. People pay a lot of money to live in the most crowded places: just think of central London or Manhattan.

And the world is not that crowded anyway. It is estimated that through settlement, infrastructure and agriculture, humans have affected a little less than 15 per cent of the world's surface.[14] With current developments in agriculture, such as the cultivation of artificial meat and hydroponics, there is every chance that we will be able to feed an expanding population on less land, and give more fields back to nature. As people become more urban, they live at higher population densities, and not only take up less space but also consume fewer resources, for example by using more public transport and services, from the post to electricity to water, that can be more efficiently delivered when people live close together.

The argument here is not for a population that grows and grows forever. Nothing can keep expanding without limits. But there is still plenty of space for humans to flourish, and indeed, as they do, they tend to take up less space and use it more efficiently. Eventually the human population is bound to stop growing and even to decline. The key argument in this book is that it should not do so yet. At some point in the future, we are likely to have technologies that will be able to substitute for a lot of human labour. But, as we will see in Chapter 8, we are not there yet. To aim for a smaller global population when the robots are still largely a dream is to build dysfunction into the world. The world's population should ideally continue growing for the foreseeable future, although not at the annual 2 per cent plus at which growth peaked 50 years ago, when much of the world was still early in its demographic transition and too few people had access to contraception. For now we need the sort of gradual, steady growth that comes when the average woman has two to three children, in a society in which very few people die before the end of their fertile years. The real problems that ageing and population decline present will be more easily handled if they are gradual. Plunging fertility rates, however, mean that they will be sudden and more disruptive.

But aiming at some absolute number of people is not really the point. 'The world was doing fine in around 1975, when it had 4 billion people,' it might be argued. 'Why should it be so terrible if it returns to 4 billion?' But what matters is the direction of travel and the consequent structure of the population. Take Japan as an example. In the mid-1960s, its total population shot upwards through the 100-million mark. Sometime in the mid-2050s, it will shoot downwards through it. The first time at 100 million, Japan had more than nine people of working age (for the purposes of this calculation, 20–65) to every one of retirement age. When it hits the same total population on the way down, three decades from now, it will have barely one and half people of working age for each retiree.

If I could choose one piece of data among the many in this book to stick in your mind, it would be this one. Because the issues of the old-age dependency ratio are the most pressing.

DEPENDENCY RATIOS

Low fertility rates, particularly when combined with longer life expectancy, mean first an ageing and then a declining population. This creates great strains on national systems of social provision as dependency ratios – the share of workers to non-workers – decline, and there are too few people to keep basic services ticking over. When a problem emerges in a particular sector, like the shortage of tanker-drivers in the UK in the autumn of 2021, this can usually be dealt with by special measures such as pay rises, or relaxations of entry requirements, or the recruitment of workers from overseas. But this is something of a case of 'whack-a-mole'. Labour can be rushed to certain sectors (easier where years of training are not required, harder in cases like medicine, where the pipeline of potential workers needs to be managed over a period of many years), but with labour being at a general premium, this only worsens shortages elsewhere.

Shortage of labour is fundamentally a demographic issue. You can raise the retirement age, but this usually leads to a bitter and sometimes violent reaction, as both Presidents Putin and Macron have discovered.[15] You can wind back the extension of tertiary education so that people start working earlier (with the potential in the long term to make your workforce less productive). But you cannot easily counteract tectonic shifts in the structure of your population.

When I joined the workforce in the UK in the mid-1980s, there were almost two people in their early twenties for every person in their late sixties. As a result, there was a fresh inflow into the workforce outweighing the number of people leaving it. That reflected the healthy fertility rate of the UK at the end of the baby boom in the early 1960s, when women were having around three children each. Today, the numbers of people in their early twenties and of those in their late sixties roughly match. The fresh inflow, thanks to the much lower fertility rate of the early years of the current century, is very much reduced, and the result is chronic labour shortages.[16] Immigration has so far been the solution for the developed world – countries like Britain have been resorting to it for decades in ever-greater quantities – but, as we will explore in Chapter 7, it has significant drawbacks, isn't possible for all countries, and is not a long-term solution for any.

The problem can most simply be captured by the old-age dependency ratio: the number of people of working age to those who are retired.[17] The exact way to calculate the ratio depends on when people start and end their working lives, but let us assume that they start at 20 and end at 65. Changes to either of these ages could help, but will make relatively little difference. Using these ages, the number of elderly to working-age people in the UK has risen from below 20 per cent in the 1950s to over 30 per cent today, and it will be approaching 60 per cent in 2100. According to the UN's 'median' estimates (there is a worse case and a better case, depending largely on fertility rates), the old-age dependency ratio will rise to 50 per cent (two workers for each retiree) in the 2050s.

The UK is far from the worst performer in this respect. In Italy, the ratio has already risen from around 15 per cent in the 1950s to around 40 per cent today, and towards the end of the century it is expected to rise to 80 per cent, which means that not far off one worker will be required to support one retiree. Financially, to keep such societies going, tax levels will have to be expropriatory. It would be hard to see why any young worker would stay in Italy under such circumstances. And even if young workers stayed, there would be far too few of them to keep the country functioning, let alone look after all the elderly. Italy is a bad case, but others are not much better. In Japan the ratio is already over 50 per cent and will also rise towards 80 per cent by the end of the century. If you take 65 as the retirement age in Japan, there will be just three workers for every two retirees by the mid-2050s. Thailand, where today there are about five workers per retiree, will fall to a similarly low level of three workers to one retiree by around 2070, in a clear case of a country getting old before it gets rich.[18]

All of this results from our laudable ability to keep people alive longer, but also from our lamentable unwillingness to reproduce ourselves. In the US, the ratio is a relatively healthy 28 per cent today (although double the level it was in the 1950s). This is thanks to the fact that fertility rates in the US have been higher than in most of the developed world for most of the last few decades. But even in the US, the old-age dependency ratio will be around 40 per cent by the mid-2040s, an enormous turnabout that will have very wide ramifications for the world's labour market and for the US itself.

In financial terms, the result is ballooning government debt, with more and more social expenditure required and fewer and fewer workers to pay for it. In the labour market it expresses itself in shortages of people to perform the jobs that need doing. In Chapter 8 we will consider whether and when technology might come to our assistance. But while we can anticipate dependency ratios shifting sharply over the decades to come, there are many jobs that need to be done, from installing new electric sockets to collecting the bins, where it is not obvious how, in the immediate future, technology is going to make existing human labour more efficient, never mind replace it altogether. The demographic problem is more certain than the potential technological solutions.

With a lack of labour to meet the needs of an ageing population in the decades to come, a certain amount of work will not get done. Political priorities and economic signals will determine what this will mean in terms of crumbling buildings, failing infrastructure or elderly, incapacitated people left to their own devices.

This demographic transition causes problems not just because of the lack of workers relative to the population, but also due to the lack of youth and creativity. As it has greyed, Japan has seen far fewer patents filed than was the case 30 or 40 years ago. At a global level, the loss of the innovation that normally flows from young people is likely to significantly reduce economic productivity. Indeed, it may already be doing so, and is perhaps partly responsible for the productivity stagnation in many advanced countries.[19] It's worth pointing out too that large communities, able to divide intellectual labour thanks to their numbers, are better at innovating. The English-speaking world produces more innovation than smaller linguistic communities because it can share its thinking so widely. The Chinese, at the cutting edge of more and more areas of invention, share a similar advantage. But can they continue to keep pumping out innovation as their younger cohorts shrink?

Of course, the 'dependency ratio' – rather than just the 'old-age dependency ratio' – should take account of all those of working age to all those not of working age: both those over the normal retirement age and those too young to work. In a modern economy, a large share of the population is in full-time education until at least age 20, and although some argue that people could work from a younger age, it seems unlikely that a modern economy could really function successfully if fewer of its young people had the benefits of a tertiary education. As the number of children shrinks, the total dependency ratio (that is the ratio of workers to both the elderly and to children) will be slightly positively affected. Yes, more capital and labour will need to go into building old-age homes and staffing them, but fewer resources will be required by nurseries and schools. Manufacturers of children's nappies can reallocate their plant and workers to making incontinence pads – Japan supposedly already uses more of the latter than the former each year.[20]

But solving the total dependency ratio by having fewer children is clearly the worst way of addressing the problem. Children do require resources from society and don't immediately put anything back, at least in economic terms. But they are the workers of the future. To invest in the care of an elderly person is compassionate and morally correct. To invest in the education and development of a young person is strengthening the seed corn for the future functioning of society. If we do succeed in increasing the fertility rate, the overall dependency ratio of society will initially worsen. Still, it would be far better to make that investment and commitment now, before elderly dependency ratios are so dire that adding the additional burden of looking after and educating more children simply becomes untenable. Having fewer children today so that we can deal more easily with the pressures of an ageing population ensures that these pressures will only continue to worsen in future.

THE LONG TERM IS NOW

For a long time, after surveying persistently low fertility rates, concerned pundits would say that 'in the long term' there would be problems. But the long term has finally arrived. The way it is manifesting itself, as we have seen, is through labour shortages across the economies of the developed world. The prime minister of Japan has spoken of societal collapse. Elon Musk foresees civilisation crumbling.[21]

It is worth reminding ourselves just how serious the situation is by looking at a few recent news reports. In Germany (sub-replacement fertility since 1970): 'Experts say the country needs about 400,000 skilled immigrants each year as its ageing workforce shrinks. The national labour agency said earlier this month that an annual analysis showed 200 out of about 1,200 professions it surveyed had labour shortages last year, up from 148 the previous year.'[22] In Japan (sub-replacement fertility since 1958): 'Japan to face 11 million worker shortfall by 2040, study finds.'[23] In China (sub-replacement fertility since 1991): 'The great people shortage hits China: the country's shrinking population is a grim omen for the rest of the world.'[24] The latest Chinese data suggest a fertility rate not much above one child per woman, meaning each cohort will be about half the size of the last – a phenomenon worsened by the fact that, in the childbearing age groups, women are under-represented because of selective abortions a generation ago. By the end of the century, China's population is forecast to fall by more than 45 per cent, and its over-65s to rise from 14 per cent to 40 per cent of the population.[25]

Since fertility rates have fallen in the last couple of decades, and since it takes a couple of decades for a newborn to enter the workplace, and as no general upturn is on the horizon – in fact, the opposite – we can only expect things to get worse. Labour shortages are showing up in every area, from restaurants and pubs cutting their opening hours because of a lack of staff, to children being taught by unqualified teachers due to a dearth of qualified educators, to infrastructure projects being abandoned or not even started for want of labour. This situation will continue and indeed deteriorate in the next couple of decades, because the underlying reason – too few people – is built into the system. If the fertility intentions of Generation Z are anything to go by, it is going to get worse still after that.

It is true that labour shortages have their upsides. Those of us who recall the years of mass unemployment in the 1980s would not wish for them to return. And a shortage of workers places upward pressure on wages. It would be no bad thing if workers across much of the industrialised world were to receive a greater share of the pie after so much of the additional product has been taken by senior management and shareholders. But once inflation is triggered, there is no guarantee that real wages will rise (that is, that wages will rise faster than inflation). Companies often find it easier to raise prices than workers do to get a pay rise. And a shortage of workers also means that many key tasks simply don't get done, which will affect everyone. In a tighter labour market, the better-off will still be able to pay for the services they require. It is those lower down the economic pecking order who will find they cannot afford a plumber or a carer in old age.

Manifestations of the toll of labour shortages in an historically low-fertility country like Japan can already be seen. Four thousand elderly people in Japan are estimated to die alone each week, and a whole industry has emerged from the need to fumigate apartments where bodies have been found long after the end of life. This is the sad ending which invariably comes at the termination of years of loneliness and solitary struggle. 'The way we die is a mirror of the way we live,' laments the chairman of a residents' council in a large housing complex outside Tokyo.[26]

In terms of economic growth, it is true that for many lower-income countries, upskilling of populations and a rise in their productivity rates will to some extent compensate for falling numbers. But it is vain to think that in countries like Germany, Italy and Japan, where a huge share of the cohort already benefits from tertiary education, this is feasible. Even in China, the days when economic growth can be fuelled by upskilling the population are already numbered: almost 60 per cent of the current cohort in China is already attending a university or similar institution.[27] For advanced countries the size of the working-age population seems to be the key determinant of economic growth.[28] And as working-age populations are set to fall in ever larger parts of the globe, the prospects for economic growth are falling too.

CAN'T WE JUST MUDDLE THROUGH?

Those worrying about the lack of children might be accused of stoking up a 'moral panic'. Yes, fertility rates are low and getting lower in an ever-growing swathe of the world, but surely things are not that bad? Societies still seem to function. The lights have not gone out yet. Aren't we just making a fuss about not very much? Only yesterday, we are told, the experts were worried about having too many people. Now they are stressing about too few.

A UK-based organisation called Population Matters, condemning a politician for raising her concerns about the low fertility rate, speaks of 'a certain amount of hysteria around these issues'. It insists that 'we need to explore positive, creative policies to deal with ageing populations'.[29] Listening to an EU official recently at a think tank session, I got the impression that it was the management of population decline, rather than its reversal, that was the goal of any demographic strategy the EU might have.

The argument goes that we can put the issue of low fertility rates in a historical context and see how they are not really so bad. In the 1920s and 1930s, fertility rates sank across Europe, falling from around three to around two in Germany and the UK, for example. Economist John Maynard Keynes was deeply concerned about the sinking birth rate and worried that a falling population would be 'very disastrous'.[30] But to general surprise, the birth rate bounced back after the Second World War across those areas where it had been most depressed in the 1930s, and sustained a reasonably high level in most such places for a couple of decades. Perhaps that could happen again without any alarm, concern, discussion or policy.

The first thing that makes it different this time is the depth to which fertility rates have fallen.[31] Interwar fertility rates even in the most advanced and urbanised countries did not fall much below two children per woman, a long way above the fertility rates of below 1.5, or even below one, experienced in many countries today.

Second, depressed fertility rates are much more widespread today than they were then. The US, the UK and Germany, countries that had all experienced very fast growth and early demographic transitions, were rare in a world in which fertility rates were still generally very high. In the less developed parts of Europe and in most of the world beyond, women were still having many children. Today, fertility rates of below 1.5 can be found in a vast and growing share of the world, including places as varied and far-flung as St Lucia, Spain and Singapore. (The low-fertility alliteration possibilities are endless: one could just as well have selected Puerto Rico, Portugal and Poland, or Jamaica, Jersey and Japan.)

And third, the period over which such demographic slumps have occurred is now far longer than the relatively brief interwar interlude. The really low fertility rates of the early and mid-1930s were probably to a large extent a reflection of the particularly difficult economic circumstances of the period, when the industrial world suffered its greatest economic crisis. In the UK, surprisingly, fertility rates were back above two by 1943.[32] By contrast, sub-replacement fertility has now persisted in some countries for more than half a century, and the impact of economic cycles is modest.

The basic demography, then, is significantly worse, with the problem of too few births more acute, more widespread and more persistent than anything we have seen before. The crisis is deeper, wider and longer than anything in the past.

WORSE FROM HERE

More alarming still, there is no end in sight. Quite the contrary. There are many reasons to think that the fertility rate of the cohort now coming to potential parenthood, Generation Z, will be lower still than that of those who preceded them.

The first reason is based on the data. It is true that fertility rates in the most advanced countries have fallen fastest for those at young ages, and slightly recovered for older ages. Far fewer teenagers are getting pregnant in most of the world than was once the case, and more women in their forties are having children: between 2004 and 2020, the fertility rate for women aged over 40 in the UK rose by almost 60 per cent. But for women aged under 20, it fell by almost 60 per cent, and for those in their early twenties, it dropped by about 33 per cent.[33] The overall effect is to depress fertility rates, since they have historically been much higher among the younger groups than the older. In the US, between 1990 and 2019, the fertility rate for teens fell by more than 70 per cent, and for those in their early twenties by more than 40 per cent. Here, too, births at older ages rose sharply, but the absolute numbers were nothing like enough to compensate for the dropping-off in the younger age groups.[34]

As a society gets wealthier and more educated, many women have degrees to complete and careers to launch before they wish to focus on having children; so we have seen not only a fall in fertility rates, but also a rise in the average age of giving birth. In the decade to 2019, it rose from under 29 to over 30 in Germany, and from 25 to 27 in Romania, for example. In the US, in just over a decade it has risen from 25 to 30, an astonishing leap in so short a time.[35] But this rise, it now appears, is fuelled not just by the long-term trend towards women delaying having children, but also by a sharp change in attitude to children among the youngest generation of potential parents, who, as well as delaying having children, in increasing numbers seem determined not to have them at all.

'Among my friends, I was a child bride, marrying at 25 and having a first baby at 29,' says an acquaintance of mine. 'None of my large group of friends has children as they approach 30.' A 2023 survey of people in the UK aged 20 to 34 found that only 55 per cent were planning to start a family at some point in the future. An astonishing 25 per cent had ruled it out altogether.[36] As a representative of the polling company put it: 'For generations, having children has just been the done thing, but it seems younger people are now deciding against this more and more.'[37] The reasons for this uncovered in the poll are familiar: a desire to enjoy life with no distractions, and concern about finances and the future. In the US, 27 per cent of Gen Zers say they do not want children.[38] The attitudes of the die-hard never-parents may soften over time, but equally, many of those who say they might or indeed would like to have children may never do so, for a whole host of reasons. One UK-based 23-year-old working for a theatre said she was concerned that the financial pressure of having children would mean she had to work for too long. 'I wanted children when I was younger but had begun to have second thoughts, then Covid hit. My partner and I both lost our jobs and I realised I'd never have the financial security to raise a family without working until I dropped.'[39] There is a general tendency to delay starting a family until an age at which the biology is more challenging. The most common age for childbearing for women born in the UK in 1975 was 31, compared to 22 for their mothers.[40] Although fertility rates only start falling materially in the early thirties, the average age of birth of 31 suggests far more women attempting to get pregnant at a later age. Biological fertility for women is estimated more or less to halve by the mid-thirties.[41]

Whatever the reasons, though, there is a generational change going on which almost guarantees that fertility rates will fall further in the coming decades rather than recover. The arrival of ubiquitous and usually free birth control certainly played its part in lowering birth rates in much of the world, but the attitude that having children at some point was the norm went largely unquestioned. Today, however, this is increasingly being questioned by the cohorts coming of age. We might consider this a good thing – people taking a more considered and reflective approach to major life events rather than just accepting previously little-questioned social norms. But if we are to avoid the problems set out in this book, it is vital for us to convey a set of pro-natal arguments.

THE DEMOGRAPHIC TRILEMMA

Once through the demographic transition, countries can have two but not three of the following: a low fertility rate and few children, ethnic homogeneity and economic dynamism. I call this the 'demographic trilemma'. If they want the first two – both to have a low total fertility rate and to retain a homogeneous society without mass immigration – like Japan they will face an ever-worsening old-age support ratio and a waning economy. If nations want a low total fertility rate and a dynamic economy, or at least aspire to economic growth, they will need to keep their old-age dependency ratios down by mass immigration – which is in any case only a temporary solution, given declining global fertility rates. Only by having a high fertility rate can a country have both a dynamic economy and avoid dependence on immigration.[42]

I worked with economist Philip Pilkington to turn this concept into numbers and to quantify what kind of trade-offs would be required. Looking at the UK data, we asked how bad the old-age dependency ratio would be if, while UK fertility rates continued to be depressed and heading towards East Asian levels, we were more or less to end immigration altogether. The answer was shocking: by the 2070s, there would be only two people of working age for every one person of retirement age. The crises of labour shortages and increasing government indebtedness would get worse, regardless of government fiscal and monetary policies. On the other hand, if the UK wished to retain its current (not particularly healthy) old-age dependency ratio and prevent any further rise in it, but still continued to let fertility rates slide, foreign-born residents would need to be heading towards half the population by the end of the century. This would require a more or less unprecedented level of immigration. And the same applies to almost everywhere in the developed world.[43]

MARKET AND STATE

There is a view that the market will sort out all these problems, and that rising real wages in an era of labour shortages are an example of this.[44] This perspective was very much in vogue on the pro-market right during the 1970s and 1980s, so it is no coincidence that I was reminded of it when sitting next to a former Thatcherite Cabinet minister at a dinner not long ago. A lively discussion was underway about immigration, with one contributor arguing that high levels of immigration were inevitable given labour shortages. The retired politician replied more or less as follows: 'Whatever the arguments for or against immigration, it is preposterous to justify it on the basis of so-called labour shortages. Every input into the economy has a price, and if the input is scarce, the price goes up until supply is stimulated and demand dampened and there is no longer a shortage.'

Markets are indeed a human institution of near-miraculous qualities that, as Adam Smith long ago pointed out, serve society through the efficient allocation of resources, even if none of the actors inside the system are privately pursuing that goal. The place of markets in human affairs, their strengths and their limitations, has been widely and intensively debated, and this is not the place for these arguments to be rehashed. But it is worth thinking through exactly what a market-based approach to the problems of demography would mean, and whether it could indeed contain a solution. For sure, there is a finite supply of capital and land and labour, and each will be partially or fully priced (depending on the appetite for government intervention) to reflect supply and demand. But the impact of a low supply of labour *relative to the population it is serving* – that is, in effect, the impact of a high old-age dependency ratio – is something relatively new. Historically we have not been used to societies or economies of this sort. And we may not like the consequences.

Imagine we lived in the perfect market society that the former Cabinet minister perhaps aspires to. There would be minimal state support for any services: everything would be run by private corporations. A shortage of labour and a rise in its price would choke off demand for it by those with the least ability to pay. The less well-off would have no access to a doctor, a dentist, a nurse or even an ambulance. Elderly and infirm, they would find nobody to care for them, and absent family members prepared to help out, they would sit neglected, waiting for death. There would be no teachers for the children of the less well-off, nor any school buildings in which to educate them.

Fortunately, we do not live in such a society. Far from it. We have a welfare state, where the government provides what are generally considered essential services. As societies age, they look more and more to the state. Older people consume more of the goods and services that electorates expect to be delivered by the state rather than by the market. They are more likely to require the services of doctors, nurses and carers, and to consume more household fuel, which we expect the state to provide or to subsidise either universally or for poorer individuals.[45] In France, the state spends over 50 per cent of GDP, and in the UK and US, not much less.[46] There are those who call for a smaller state, particularly in the Anglosphere, and promise lower taxes. But this is an unrealistic aspiration given our current demographic condition. More and more will be expected of the state as ageing populations require higher levels of social care and healthcare and a larger share of national spend through pensions. The state in the developed world, which is expected to provide a wide array of services, will find itself increasingly hard-pressed as it becomes obliged to deploy and to finance an ever-growing share of the shrinking national labour force to provide the services its electorates demand.

The financial result of this will be a combination of rising taxes and growing government debt. We have already noted how countries with the worst and longest-standing ageing problem, like Japan, Greece and Italy, tend to have the worst levels of government debt to GDP among the rich countries. In Japan debt has reached well over 200 per cent, more than twice the level of the UK.[47] What societies demand from the state, and what they are prepared to pay for this in the form of taxes, are not the same thing. Expectations both of state provision and of an acceptable level of taxation were set in an era when young taxpayers were burgeoning and those requiring pensions and intense healthcare were relatively few and far between. Although ageing changes this equation, it is not something that electorates understand, or want to understand. They still want to keep and freely spend most of their income and savings, while expecting the kind of provision outlined above. The result is that governments resort to borrowing to fill the gap.

In some ways this works rather well. Until the rise in inflation and interest rates in the early 2020s, governments could borrow at remarkably low interest rates. The yield on Japanese government bonds in August 2023 was still negative for a year, and well below 1 per cent for ten years.[48] In part this reflects the deflationary expectations of investors, a function of a demographically driven pessimism about the prospects of the Japanese economy. It also reflects the fact that Japanese investors, being old, are looking for the safest class of assets available and are happy for now to park their savings with the government rather than risk them in local equity markets that have delivered decades of lacklustre and even disastrous performance.[49] The Japanese saver, at least, is prepared to fund the deficits of the Japanese government. And a great deal of Japanese government debt has simply been bought by the Bank of Japan, paid for by a long-standing and vast programme of quantitative easing.[50]

But bankruptcy, as a character in an Ernest Hemingway novel famously said, happens gradually then suddenly. There is no way to be certain when the printing of money to finance debt will trigger inflation. The inflation of the early 2020s in many countries, coming after years of fast money-printing, was not generally expected. And panics over the reliability of a debtor's creditworthiness can likewise happen quite suddenly. A UK government perceived as profligate and incompetent saw bond yields rise from a little under 2 per cent to nearly 4.5 per cent in the space of a few weeks in the late summer and early autumn of 2022.[51] The result was a political crisis and a change of leadership. But these are potentially mere blips compared with the sorts of disasters that could occur if and when private and professional investors decide that they do not trust governments with their money and are no longer prepared to continue financing government debt through the bond markets.

With the prospect of endlessly mounting government debt, such an occurrence cannot be discounted with any more certainty than its timing can be predicted. But if and when it happens, the entire economic and political system could collapse. In the summer of 2023, one of the major ratings agencies downgraded US government debt, traditionally seen as the absolute last word in risk-free assets.[52] Credit rating agencies are linking a loss of faith in government finance with ageing. 'In the past, demographics were a medium- to long-term consideration. Now, the future is with us and already hitting sovereign credit profiles,' says a representative of Moody's. 'While demographics are slow-moving, the problem is becoming more urgent. We are well into the adverse effects in many countries, and they are only growing,' says a senior executive at Fitch.[53] Without doubt there are many complex reasons for this, but the underlying fiscal problems of the US and the rest of the developed world would look very different if they had the young and growing populations that characterised these countries 30 or 40 years ago.

When the financial credibility of the banks was shot in 2008, only the action of governments, the ultimate source of creditworthiness, could save the system. If and when the financial credibility of governments collapses, there will be no final backstop available. The last time there was a meltdown on anything like such a scale, the consequence was a rising tide of communism, fascism and war. The precise form the crisis will take next time is anyone's guess, but it is unlikely to be pleasant. Even if such a financial Armageddon never takes place, we need a population revival to return the developed countries to the kind of demographic condition they were in 50 years ago. And even if we were to fix the fertility rate tomorrow, that would not happen for decades to come.

GETTING THROUGH THE BOTTLENECK

An alternative argument proposing that this is all a panic is to talk of this being just another population bottleneck of the sort humans and indeed other species have frequently experienced before. In the past, it was famine or war or pestilence that reduced human populations, leaving behind a smaller community that in due course regenerated itself. This time the crisis will not be kicked off by some external catastrophe but through a self-inflicted process whereby those who do not wish to have children gently disappear into history, while those inclined towards pro-natalism create the descendants to eventually take their place.

This may turn out to be the case, but there are a number of reasons to be sceptical or concerned. First, this only works if the surviving populations have some kind of immunity to the low-fertility preferences of those whose lines have not continued. When the Black Death struck, for example, the survivors were best-placed to survive further waves of the disease through a process of natural selection, and they passed on their genes to future generations. But this analogy only works if we think that a preference for having more children is genetic – that those lacking such genes would in the past have had children anyway, due to a lack of reliable, affordable contraception, or to social pressures, so up to now such a genetic disposition has not been selected against. Free now to avoid conception and with a new social environment that no longer promotes child-bearing, people lacking the pro-natal gene or gene complex will not have children and only those with pro-natal genetic predispositions will do so. Future generations would then be more likely to carry it, and fertility rates would perk up as they expressed their preferences through having more children. This could conceivably be the case, but while there is some evidence of a genetic link to early childbearing, it is neither strong nor decisive.[54] So pro-natalism is unlikely to be able to rely on it.

Alternatively, the bottleneck could be a cultural rather than a biological one. Even if there is no genetic predisposition to pro-natalism, it is the case, as we have seen, that certain groups formed around ideologies, and particularly around religions, are pro-natally disposed. The urban liberal hipsters will all die out and fail to pass on their culture, and the only people left will be those who have children and inculcate in them a desire to have their own children in turn. High-fertility cultures will produce offspring and instil in them pro-natal values that they will perpetuate, and thus the global fertility rate will rise again.

But relying on cultural pro-natalism has its limitations. The system does not work unless the community is able to retain its own and has a low level of attrition. A religion that attracts highly pro-natal individuals and cultivates high-fertility practice but whose children do not in turn stay within the fold and have a large number of children themselves will remain forever on the demographic fringes. Only if most of each cohort stay within the religion and in turn have large numbers of children themselves will they enjoy the effect of compound growth. Indeed, this has driven up the number of Amish tenfold since the 1950s, although today the Amish are still small in number. To become a big enough group to impact the overall level of fertility within the US, they would have to grow tenfold and tenfold again, at which point they would still represent only about 10 per cent of the US population at today's size. It will only be at that stage that their high-fertility choices will start to register at the level of national data. To do this, and multiply

100-fold from today's level, they will have to prevent the bulk of their young drifting off to join the majority of society with its low-fertility norms. And they will have to do so over a very long period of time, perhaps 150 years, at which point the nature of the society into which they are aspiring *not* to assimilate will be incalculably different from today's.

But we have to ask whether, even if this were possible, we would really want such a society to exist in which a healthy fertility rate has only been achieved by the adherence of ever-larger numbers of people to beliefs and lifestyles that can be accommodated for minority movements but will be far more challenging if and when they become demographically pre-dominant. Israel is already starting to wrestle with this as the number of Haredim has grown and now represents more than 10 per cent of society. These groups tend to resist the types of education and professions that allow modern societies to function. A friend of mine is a dentist in London, and most of his clients are Haredi Jews. Although there are strictly Orthodox Jews who are in medicine and allied professions, Haredim would generally prefer their children to avoid the type of biological and medical education required to become dentists themselves, so they are reliant on the services of my friend, as they are on the services of other people pursuing professions they do not wish to qualify for and practise. If such people were to become statistically mainstream, it would not be easy to keep the lights on and basic services flowing. And while I have been quite content to live in a London neighbourhood that has grown increasingly Haredi over the three decades I have been there, I am far from sure I would wish to live in a country where people with such traditional lifestyles formed the majority of the electorate.

Besides, such groups are also better able to function when they are small minorities living under a larger liberal umbrella. If they become very numerous, they may find it difficult to maintain a society with others who have radically different attitudes. I bumped into an acquaintance recently who had left the high-fertility religious group into which he had been born. He had married at 18 and he and his wife had had two children in quick succession before he abandoned the marriage and the group. He has since been making his way in secular society, for which his education and even his language skills did not properly equip him. I told him about the book I was writing. 'Yes, you must write such a book and spread the word,' he said to me. 'Otherwise only the fanatics will have children and what sort of society would we live in then?' However much anti-natal liberals may dislike pro-natalists, the feelings are not reciprocated. On the contrary. We understand how the societies we live in are reliant on people with liberal attitudes, and their outlook, lifestyles and tolerance. Our appeal is for them to bear and rear the next generation of themselves. We need them.

It would be sad and possibly catastrophic to lose the liberals whose norms allow us to hold together societies of extraordinary diversity. It would be heartbreaking too to lose those cultures and civilisations that, for whatever reason, are not nurturing the high-fertility communities of the future, ensuring that they will eventually cease to exist as viable nations. My knowledge and appreciation of Korean culture is limited, despite my travels in that country, but for many people, the loss of the language and civilisation that is Korea, with its unique history, would be tragic. The same goes for Japan and the Japanese. The barely 3 million people of Jamaica will not take long to find that their population is unviable at current fertility rates, meaning the loss of another culture valued for its own sake and on its own terms by its own people and many millions of others around the world. Ditto Italians. Whether K-pop, reggae or opera is your taste, so many of the multiple and diverse pieces in the glorious mosaic that is humanity stand to be lost.

Even if we are just about to go through a bottleneck, and even if we do come out the other side with at least some nations and ethnic groups still alive, built on societies popu-lated by child-loving people (whether for biological or cultural reasons), it will not be an easy bottleneck to traverse. Much of value will be lost in the process. To leave this problem to history to resolve would be a foolhardy gamble.

GROUNDS FOR HOPE

For me, as for so many people, having children and now grand-children has been among the greatest joys of my life, and the good news is that in much of the world, despite shifting ide-ologies and preferences, people still want children, or at least say that they do. A recent survey of women in the UK aged 18–24 found that over 90 per cent wanted to have children and the average number to which they aspired was 2.25.[55] The bad news is that these hopes are not being realised. Given current UK fertility rates, there is a gap between aspiration and the reality of three-quarters of a child. In the US, the gap is around half a child.[56] Behind those rather weird statistics (talking of children in fractional terms seems strange but is essential for demographers) lie many disappointed hopes and much heartache. Another survey shows that, for an older cohort looking back, more than three times as many people in the UK aged 55–64 wish they had had more children than they did than wish they had had fewer.[57] The personal reasons for having children – the fundamental drive to procreate, to create a family – are not dead. Societies across the world need to tap more effectively into that desire. But before we think about how they can do so, we need to understand better why, despite the continuing desire for children, fertility rates have fallen so low.

2

PATHS TO LOW FERTILITY

FROM PRE-MODERN TO MODERN: DRIVERS OF THE DEMOGRAPHIC TRANSITION

THE classic model of human demography, which fits some places more perfectly than others but almost all pretty well, suggests that in the beginning people were breeding like rabbits and dying like flies. And this was true for the vast bulk of human history. In most places, a quarter or a third of children died before their first birthday, and the majority of people died before completing their fertile years. When circumstances were favourable, with good weather, bumper crops, and no pandemics or wars, the population would surge upwards, as fewer people died. Then it would fall back as some calamity or other struck the community.

In Europe, the early and high Middle Ages saw major population growth before the numbers were knocked back by the cold weather and bad harvests of the 1310s and by the Black Death from the 1340s onwards. Another great setback occurred during the first half of the seventeenth century, particularly in Germany, when up to a third of the population died during the Thirty Years War. Similar forward and backward motions are recorded in China, with plagues and conflicts punctuating population growth. In some places it is reckoned that populations took centuries to return to their pre-catastrophe highs. Ireland's potato blight of the 1840s not only caused about a million deaths but set off a pattern of emigration that was so intense and continued for so long that despite decades of high fertility in the intervening years, the population has still not returned to its former peak.[1]

Globally, population inched forward, taking from around the year AD 1 to around 1800 to grow from a quarter of a billion to a billion.[2] This meant an average annual growth rate of less than one-twentieth of what the world managed in 1964, for example.

The appallingly high level of infant mortality in all pre-modern societies is brought home to us when we read the biographies of famous and often materially well-off people in earlier centuries. Queen Anne (r. 1702–14) had not a single surviving child from 17 pregnancies – and she herself died just short of age 50. Conditions were better in Victorian England, but this still did not prevent someone as distinguished and financially comfortable as Charles Darwin losing three of his ten offspring in childhood or infancy. Progress was made in the nineteenth century with falls in infant mortality gathering pace towards its end and particularly in the early years of the twentieth, but Britain was, in demography as in most things, ahead of the Continent at that stage.

The music of Gustav Mahler, who was born and brought up in Bohemia in what was then the Austro-Hungarian Empire, is haunted by a childhood scarred by being one of six surviving children out of a total of 12. One of his own two children died

45

at the age of four, and that was in the early twentieth century when infant mortality was starting to fall strongly in the more advanced parts of Europe. The deaths of children, the losses of sons and daughters at a young age, and of siblings in one's own childhood, was quite normal in a way we now find hard to comprehend.

This demographic regime, captured by English clergyman Thomas Malthus in his *Essay on the Principle of Population* (1798 and subsequent revised editions), meant that for most of history, most of humanity was living at or close to the edge of existence, generally in a state of material misery. But the industrial revolution and the processes of what can be described as 'modernity' eventually changed all that. First in the UK, then across Europe, and finally across the world, mortality rates fell and populations grew as even rudimentary improvements in the quantity and purity of food, the cleanliness of water, and the provision of public health measures and medical knowledge pushed back death. With plenty of births but fewer deaths, populations surged. Eventually, richer, more educated and more urban populations became able to control their own fertility and chose to reduce it. This came to be known as the 'demographic transition': first falling mortality and a growing population, then falling fertility and a stabilising population.[3]

In more developed societies with healthcare systems and government programmes, people can more easily access contraceptives. Better educated, they are more able to use them effectively. But it is not just a question of the *ability* to reduce fertility; there is also the question of *will* and *motive*. Classic demographic transition theory suggests that in a high infant-mortality scenario, people realise, consciously or not, that they need to have a large number of children just to ensure a couple of survivors. In a high-mortality society, a fertility rate of only two will mean rapid extinction. Six children at least are required for a steady-state population, because two will likely die in infancy and another two will die before they can complete their own fertility.

Once improved conditions mean that infant mortality falls, it takes a while before childbearing habits adapt. We can see this in Guinea, in West Africa, where the infant mortality rate has fallen steadily from more than one in five to fewer than one in 15 since the early 1960s. But it was only from the early 1990s that the fertility rate started to drop, from around 6.5 then to around 4.5 now. Over the same period infant mortality has fallen sharply in Denmark too, from about one in 50 to about one in 300 since the early 1960s, although throughout this period and long before, infant mortality in Denmark was too low and high infant mortality was too far back in the collective memory for people to have extra children to counteract the loss of children.[4]

There is a complementary economic explanation as to why people in poor agricultural societies have many children, while urban and industrial (and post-industrial) folk have fewer. In rural Guinea, an extra child, initially fed exclusively from his or her mother's breast and not expected to be the recipient of lots of special baby equipment, imposes little cost on the family. At some point in early childhood, he or she can be put to some economically useful activity in the home or in the field. Education is hard to access and is of questionable economic value in any case, given the opportunities available. Perhaps the flow of economic value is still from the parent to the child: even in hunter-gatherer societies this probably remains the case.[5] But overall, the flow is modest. Children are not a significant drain on short-term resources in poor rural societies, so incentives to reduce their number (as well as, often, the means to control fertility) are limited or do not exist at all. In modern urban living, by contrast, children are expensive to rear and to educate but, with the right investment and qualifications, can potentially earn a high salary decades after their birth.

This is why it might make sense for a couple in a remote Guinean village to have many children, while city dwellers in the capital Conakry want to have fewer. In Conakry, poor though it may be, wages are higher than in the countryside. Education levels are higher. People are more likely to watch television and have access to the internet. They are more likely to have access to birth control and are more likely to be within reach of medical care, albeit rudimentary, to help keep alive those children they do have. And they are more likely to be able to put their children through school and for that schooling in due course to pay off when it comes to entering the workforce. For similar reasons this is why, for example, people living in Kolkata in West Bengal in India have half the fertility rate of the state as a whole.[6] Or why women in Addis Ababa have half the number of children compared to women in Ethiopia overall.[7] In poor agricultural societies, wealth might at some point start to flow from children, who provide a useful pair of hands in the field from an early age, to parents. In developed urban societies, with expensive childcare and education, wealth flows the other way, in large quantities and for a long time, which incentivises parents to have fewer children in the town.[8] In addition to the financial incentives, there is the compounding effect that urban women tend to be more educated and to have easier access to contraception. So as well as the will, there is also the ability to translate a desire for fewer children into reality as people become more urban, wealthy and educated.

AFRICA: DEMOGRAPHIC HISTORY IN PROGRESS

Most of the world has now largely passed through its demographic transition with relatively long life expectancy and low fertility rates. This is true even of countries considered poor until quite recently: both Mexico and Bangladesh, for example, have life expectancy beyond 70 years and fertility rates below replacement.

The one part of the world still working its way through the transition is Africa, the continent that is least economically developed. Until not that long ago, much of Africa had not even started on the transition, but almost everywhere, life expectancy is now lengthening and in most places fertility is falling. It is worth spending some time examining this last place on the planet where the traditional processes of demography are still in progress. But as you would expect in an area of such size and variety, the different parts of the continent are at very different points on their demographic journeys.

If Africa is the global exception, the last redoubt of high fertility, then it contains exceptions within itself as the exception. The picture across the continent is far from uniform. Let's start north of the Sahara. The countries of the southern Mediterranean shore, which are overwhelmingly Islamic in religion and predominantly Arabic in language, are culturally and economically distinct from the rest of the continent, where a mix of Christianity, Islam and animism coexist, and where languages are highly varied but predominantly part of the Bantu family. North Africa may appear poor from the perspective of Europe, but viewed from the south, the opposite is the case. All the countries from Morocco to Egypt have a per capita GDP of USD 3,000 to USD 5,000, with the exception of oil-rich Libya, where it is more than USD 6,500. The GDP per capita level for most North African countries is around a tenth of the per capita GDP of most members of the EU. But it is seven times higher than that of a really poor sub-Saharan African country like Sierra Leone, and more than three times higher than that of a more successful one like Ethiopia.[9]

So it should come as no surprise that the African countries of the Mediterranean littoral are not like the rest of the continent demographically. They all had very high fertility rates until relatively recently, but they have all seen fertility fall quite sharply to moderate levels in the past few decades, to between two and three children per woman. In Tunisia, fertility is barely at replacement level, and its president has even expressed concern about the country being swamped by sub-Saharans. After his declaration that the 'goal' of this immigration was to untether Tunisia from its Arab roots, you could even say that 'replacement theory' – the conspiratorial idea normally associated with white supremacists in Europe and North America that there is a plot to replace the indigenous population with an imported and alien one – has now reached the Arab world.[10]

At the opposite end of the continent, a similar story can be told, albeit with a slightly different twist. Like the countries north of the Sahara, South Africa has been relatively successful economically – more so, in fact, with a per capita income of around USD 7,000. Again, this might not seem much from the perspective of the developed world, but from the viewpoint of most of Africa, it represents real material wealth. Because of its relatively advanced socio-economic condition, you would expect South Africa to be ahead of the rest of the continent demographically, and so it is: for nearly 30 years South Africa has enjoyed a moderate fertility rate of two to three children per woman, similar to that of North Africa.

What is notable in the case of South Africa is that its low fertility habits have been catchy, and have spread especially to its immediate neighbours. Relatively low fertility is no longer just a *South* African phenomenon but increasingly a *southern* African one. Women in Botswana are already having fewer than three children each, as are those in Eswatini (previously Swaziland). Their sisters in Namibia and Lesotho are not far behind. To some extent this reflects the general economic and social progress these countries are making. But it also shows the extent of demographic 'overshoot', with falls in fertility running ahead of development, particularly in the case of Lesotho, which is still among the continent's poorer relations. It is too early to say for sure whether these neighbours will, like South Africa, follow the path towards, but not to below, replacement fertility. But there are indications that this will be the case, because like South Africa, they have tended to see a flattening off rather than a precipitous drop once fertility rates fell below three.

The story, therefore, of the continent's northern and southern nations is one of a great reduction in fertility and its stabilisation at a sustainable level generally in line with, but in some cases ahead of, social and economic development. In most cases, it has been accompanied by government campaigns to popularise and spread contraception, often backed by foreign donors or international aid agencies. For the rest of Africa, the picture is different, but again by no means uniform.

The populations of East Africa are growing fast, but these are also some of the countries managing most rapidly to bring their fertility rates under control. This can be seen in a country like Rwanda, a leader on the continent in many ways. Since the 1980s, its fertility rate has halved while income per capita has more than doubled; the one cannot really be envisaged without the other.[11] If Rwandan women were still having eight and not four children, the country would doubtless be more populous, but it would be less, not more, influential.

In Uganda and Tanzania there have been calls by some politicians at various times to keep fertility rates high – a phenomenon we might call 'hyper-natalism', the desire to retain exceptionally high fertility rates and resist the progress of the demographic transition in poor countries. Despite this, both countries are now experiencing falling fertility. But Kenya is well ahead in this respect. Kenya's total fertility rate took a while to drop – it was still around seven in the mid-1980s – but now it is half that, and continuing to fall. Kenya has been helped on its smooth path by more or less consistent family-planning policies from the government.

Likewise, in Ethiopia, fertility rates remain high at around four but are still much lower than a few decades ago. Nairobi and Addis Ababa, Kenya and Ethiopia's respective capitals, have more or less reached replacement levels, and as these two East African giants become more urban, we can be sure that more declines in fertility rates lie ahead. 'Women stay longer in school, the standard of living is increasing so people don't want to have too many children and more importantly, family planning is becoming more popular,' says a UN official. 'My husband is the one who took me to college,' says one woman taking advantage of the programme the UN provides. 'I wanted a better life for my children.'[12] These are sentiments familiar across much of the world where family planning has become the norm.

While the countries of East Africa have years of population growth ahead of them even as their fertility rates fall, and as those of the north and south already have some kind of population stability in sight, the situation in the centre and west of Africa remains different. From the tropical forests of the Democratic Republic of Congo to the deserts of the Mauritanian coast we find the last true strongholds of unremittingly high fertility rates on the planet. A classic demographic transition is taking place in Africa, but its countries are at different stages. Kenya has a fertility rate below 3.5.[13] Its per capita income is now above USD 5,000, and its life expectancy is over 65 years.[14] Over 80 per cent of its adults are literate.[15] By contrast, the women of the Central African Republic are still having more than six children each, as they have been for decades, and the country's other data also suggest that it is correspondingly behind in the race for development: per capita income is a fraction of Kenya's, life expectancy is under 55, and not much more than a third of adults are literate.[16] These are exactly the characteristics of a country where we would expect to find persistently high fertility rates.

Nigeria, however, is a case of its own, and is Africa's population giant. With more than 200 million people, it is home to about one in six sub-Saharans. It appears to be rich, with per capita income not far off South African levels, but it is extremely unequal, as its oil wealth directly benefits only a small slice of the population. Almost a third of its women remain illiterate.[17] As socio-economic development has stalled, so too has demographic progress. It has taken Nigeria 30 years to get its fertility rate down from 6.3 to 5.3. Iran and China, by contrast, experienced three times the drop in half and a third of the time, respectively.

But Nigeria itself is far from uniform. There are significant ethnic differences in Nigeria, with Fulani and Hausa citizens, predominantly Muslim and living in the less developed north, having eight children, while Igbo and Yoruba, southerners and respectively Christians and mixed Christians/Muslims, pro-ducing closer to four.[18] Education and the use of contraceptives are greater in the south. Supercharged fertility has helped boost the Muslim share of the population from a little over a third at independence in 1960 to a little over a half today.[19] The fertility rate in Lagos, the predominantly Christian Nigerian megalopolis of around 15 million people, is high for an urban area at around 3.5, but this is still almost two whole children below the national average.[20]

Nigeria matters because of its size, but it is not the most extreme case of high fertility. The country with the highest fertility rate in the world is next-door Niger, where it remains a little below seven.[21] Niger lacks Nigeria's oil resource and its great cities (its capital, Niamey, has about one-tenth of the people living in Lagos, and the share of its population which is urban is 17 per cent versus Nigeria's roughly 50 per cent).[22] It is, like high-fertility northern Nigeria, overwhelmingly Muslim. Its literacy rate is barely 60 per cent of Nigeria's.[23] So we should not be surprised that its fertility rate is higher and we can expect it to fall more slowly.

Although fertility data are cut-and-dried, being the number of children women actually *have*, a less precise measurement, but still a significant one, is the number of children they *want*, or say they want. Cultures are diverse, and the exact meaning of questions in different languages can be subtly nuanced, so we cannot treat comparative measurements of desired family size with quite the scientific precision of measurements of actual family size. But if we want to understand what the world's last high-fertility countries can teach an increasingly low-fertility world, we should take them into account.

You might think that women would generally want to reduce the number of children they bring into the world in places where they are still, on average, having five or six. Some people think of Africa as a continent full of young women desperate to escape the demands of their pro-natalist husbands and partners, and yearning for birth control, if only it could be made available. There is certainly plenty of anecdote to support such a view. 'If you tell your husband that you don't want a large family, he will just go and marry another woman,' says the mother of eight children in a fishing village in the south of Benin (where they have a total fertility rate of five). 'It's a lot of pressure. Our husbands love children and large families… I've had too many babies… I feel sicker and weaker. I suffer illnesses, like hypertension. I get headaches and vertigo and fatigue.' Her husband views things differently: 'You need a lot of babies because you never know how many are going to live and how many are going to die. What if we had only two babies and both died?'[24]

It is just as easy, however, to cite anecdotes to the contrary, suggesting that women are satisfied with or at least resigned to bearing large families. 'I have ten children,' says a woman in

Kano, Nigeria. 'It is the will of God,' she explains as children and grandchildren scramble around her.[25]

The data suggest that indeed it may not be the case that the continent is full of women longing to limit the size of their families. A widespread academic survey in more than 30 African countries showed two-thirds of women wanting more children, not fewer. Notably, the country where they were least likely to express this desire was relatively low-fertility South Africa, while the place they were most likely to want more children was fertility-supercharged Niger. The same study showed that the desire for more children declined, as we would expect, as women's levels of education and workforce participation rose. Access to television and the media also correlated with a declining desire for a large family.[26] Overall, women in East Africa want a child and a half less than their sisters in central and West Africa.[27] In Ethiopia, where the population is increasingly urbanised and literate, the number of children desired per woman has sunk from around 7.5 to around four since the 1980s, and actual fertility has fallen in lockstep. (The same has happened in India.)[28] Broadly it would seem that the same conditions that bring down the number of children people want also reduce the number of children they have.

AFTER REACHING DENMARK: POST-MODERN FERTILITY RATES

The political theorist Francis Fukuyama suggested that Denmark was the inevitable fate, or at least the inevitable aspiration, of all countries and peoples. Who would not want stable, democratic order, respect for human rights, low levels of crime, and high levels of income and human development? Whatever the merits of his ideas from a more general political and economic perspective, we are all getting to Denmark demographically.[29] Alongside economic development, and sometimes bounding ahead of it, countries as different as Colombia and Cambodia, Morocco and Myanmar, regardless of their political status, religious or cultural affiliations, are all converging on the model of low fertility and rising life expectancy that Denmark typifies. When it comes to key demographic metrics, the world more closely resembles Denmark with every passing year.

This is the story of modernisation, and it is one that any reasonable person should wish to celebrate. Pro-natalism needs to be clearly and distinctly differentiated from the simple *natalism* of societies where low levels of education and development, and often patriarchal social systems, mean that women have six or seven children on average and little say in the matter. That is demographic prehistory, and the sooner it is consigned to the past, the better.

But demographic history, the process of transition, does not end when we get to Denmark. Indeed, it did not end in Denmark itself. Along with the rest of Scandinavia, Denmark has not suffered the extremely low fertility rates of southern and eastern Europe, never mind East Asia, but, like much of the developed world, its fertility rate has still not been above replacement level for more than 50 years. It tailed off rapidly from the late 1960s, as happened in much of Europe and North America, after a late flourishing of the post-war baby boom in the mid-1960s.

Proponents of the 'second demographic transition' theory suggest that in Denmark and other countries of similar levels of development, the population has now settled into an era when the pursuit of personal projects, the breakdown of traditional family structures and a general cultural shift mean that fertility rates are bound to be below replacement level, necessitating mass immigration from countries at an earlier stage and therefore resulting in rapid ethnic change.[30]

However, the story is not just one of progressive social norms creating low fertility. For example, some of the lowest fertility rates are in countries such as Greece and Korea, where cohabitation outside marriage remains fairly rare and births outside wedlock are relatively few.[31] The simple correlation of a country being 'socially progressive' on the one hand (with low rates of marriage, late marriage, high rates of childbirth outside wedlock, cohabitation as a norm, and high levels of rights for women in the workplace and the home) and having a low fertility rate on the other, simply does not work any more. And here we must find a cause for hope. Because it means that even if the whole world is indeed moving in the direction of Denmark when it comes to attitudes to women and the family, it need not necessarily be moving towards ultra-low fertility rates. Up to a point in economic development, fertility rates are bound to fall, as we see still happening in much of sub-Saharan Africa. But once you get beyond that point – once society is reasonably urban and generally literate and in which access to contraception is general – then it is culture rather than material conditions that determines whether you have a moderate or low fertility rate.

Now that much of the world is through its (first) demographic transition – now that high levels of income, urbanisation and education are normal if not universal throughout so much of the globe, and now that contraception is so widely available in so many places – the fact is that fertility rates are plummeting, and whether they are very low, as in Korea and Greece, or just low, as in Denmark and the US, they are too low for long-term sustainability. There are exceptions, but for now our task is to try to figure out why the rule is that once a nation comes even within sight of Danish levels of development, its fertility rate tends to dive below replacement level and stay there.

The relationship between low fertility and family size is not as simple as a rising wave of childlessness, as has been suggested. It is not just that more women are having no children: fewer who do have families are having large ones. About 18 per cent of women born in the mid-1970s in England and Wales remain childless as they reach the end of their fertile years, which is not very different from the cohorts born in the 1950s and 1960s.[32] The rate of childlessness in Japan is nearly three times as high as that in Ukraine even though Japan has a slightly higher fertility rate. Spain and Portugal have similar fertility rates, but again Spain has three times as many childless women as Portugal.[33] So the distribution of children across the cohort of childbearing women may vary even where the total fertility rate does not.

But this is to consider the share of childless women only at the end of their fertile years, a somewhat backward-looking measure in that it cannot (more or less) definitively be determined for a cohort until it reaches its mid-forties. Clearly there is a trend towards greater childlessness. Unless today's cohort of thirty-somethings pull off a very big surprise and have significantly more children than we would expect even from the clear rising trend to have more children very late, we can expect a significantly increasing share of women to end their fertile years with no children at all.

With low fertility being an ever-wider phenomenon, we assume either that it must have a single set of causes, or that perhaps there is some deep-rooted causality which manifests itself differently in different places. This is a difficult and complex subject: whenever you think you have nailed some fundamental cause, an exception will present itself. Expensive housing? You can cite plenty of places with low fertility despite cheap housing. Unaffordable and inaccessible childcare? Likewise. One very thoughtful commentator says: 'Confronting demographic decline means dealing with drug and alcohol abuse, because drug and alcohol abuse contributes to criminality, to unemployment, to non-marriageability.'[34] But this is a very American perspective. Some of the lowest fertility rates in the world are in places from Japan to Spain with very little drug and alcohol abuse.[35]

It was material advance that drove fertility rates to fall towards replacement. In some places this is still occurring. But for the already-developed world and even for some of the not-yet-fully developed world, material advance is no longer the answer, and there are a number of other factors that are dragging fertility rates below replacement or which at least correlate strongly with low fertility. We will now take a look at these.

3

EXPLAINING TODAY'S
LOW FERTILITY

A DEMOGRAPHER'S definition of fertility is the number of children people actually have. A biologist's definition of fertility is the ability of people to have children. Biological issues are a potential constraint on demographic fertility: people who want to have children but who can't for medical reasons.

There has been much talk in recent times of falling sperm count, and this could theoretically (and eventually) cause humanity a demographic problem.[1] However, the evidence to date is that most couples of an appropriate age and with reasonably regular effort are able to conceive within a fairly short period.[2] As attempted family formation is delayed and conception attempted at later ages, difficulties in conception are likely to go up and there will be more requirement for IVF and other forms of technological intervention. The technology is progressing. But at the moment it's a small minority of people who need it, and it isn't contributing much to the low and falling (demographic) fertility. To understand why fertility is so low in so much of today's world, we must turn to a number of features of contemporary society rather than biology.

SECULARISM

Nobody decides not to have children simply because they are secular, but a non-religious outlook is certainly more compatible with other ideologies that push people to have small families or none at all. So while a lack of religious faith does not lead directly to no or few children, and plenty of non-believers have quite large families, there seems to be a strong connection between societies losing their faith and losing their fertility. Once ways of people controlling their own fertility become common, the difference religion makes starts to show up. The French seem to have been early adopters of family-planning techniques and the difference in fertility rates between areas where Catholicism was strong and elsewhere could be seen in the nineteenth century. According to one innovative study, Catholic Brittany went through a fertility decline a whole century or more after relatively secular Provence, a testimony to the delaying impact of religion on the decline in birth rates.[3] Religion appears to have made the difference in nineteenth- and early twentieth-century France of almost one and three-quarter children per woman.[4]

When it comes to the contemporary world, in the US it turns out that whereas the fertility rate of those who attend religious services weekly has held consistently at about replacement rate for the past 40 years, for those who consider themselves non-religious, fertility has fallen to such an extent that now the gap between the two groups is about four-fifths of a child (2.1 versus 1.3). This difference is enormous in terms of what it means for the future of society and for whether a population can keep its head above water or will sink fast. Those who are somewhat religious and attend services from time to time, but not weekly, fall somewhere in between the weekly attenders and the non-attenders when it comes to fertility. The overall decline in American levels of fertility is largely explicable not by a drop in the fertility rate of the religious or of the non-religious but rather by the rise in the share of the non-religious in the population as a whole.[5] The ultra-high fertility rate of the extremely religious in the US, whether Christian or Jewish, is well known. But what is often not appreciated is the moderate but positive fertility premium of those who just attend their place of worship weekly rather than those who steer clear of such places altogether. As religious affiliation falls, so too does fertility. Self-identifying Christians have fallen as a share of the US population from three-quarters to less than two-thirds in the past ten years, while those who identify as having no religion have increased from fewer than 20 per cent to almost 30 per cent in the past decade or so.[6]

The tendency for religion to correlate positively with fertility persists beyond the US. In the UK, practising Catholic women have more than half a child, and practising Protestant women almost a third of a child, more than non-religious women. In France, the gap between Catholic and non-practising women is half a child.[7] In Spain, women who attended Mass as children have more than half a child more than women who did not.[8] In Israel, more than 80 per cent of ultra-Orthodox women have three children or more; the figure is 53 per cent for those who define themselves as 'religious' and only 22 per cent for those who say they are wholly secular. Some 42 per cent of people defining themselves as secular have no children, but fewer than 9 per cent of the ultra-Orthodox are childless.[9] The data from the Islamic world are less clear, but there is nonetheless strong evidence from countries as distant and diverse as Indonesia and Egypt that faith and fertility are positively correlated for Muslims, just as they are for Christians and Jews elsewhere.[10]

But that seems to be relevant only to the Abrahamic religions. Buddhist countries from Thailand to Korea, by contrast, have very low levels of fertility for their stage of development. We might expect the more religious within Buddhist countries to have a higher fertility rate than the unaffiliated, but studies from countries as diverse as Singapore, Mongolia, Korea and Japan have found that a stronger attachment to Buddhism does not mean more children.[11] The same holds true for Hinduism in India.

So it is within the Abrahamic world alone that there is a correlation of religious affiliation, belief and practice with fertility. The obvious explanation is simply that, as we have seen, people who are religious follow teachings that in some way encourage them to have larger families. But there may be more to it than simply following the letter of the religious law. Another explanation, which could be complementary rather than an alternative, is that religious women, or at least those who regularly attend religious services, are part of a social network and have social capital, which makes bringing up children somewhat easier, although this only seems to apply to religions which are explicitly pro-natal. 'When I was raising my children,' I was told by Clara, a Londoner, full-time worker, mother of three and regular attender of religious services, 'having the advice, friendship and when required assistance of other women at a similar stage in their lives was enormously helpful. We could child-mind in emergencies and generally help each other out. That kind of network might have been possible outside the context of a religious community, but it is much less likely that I would have found it. And without it, coping with three kids and a full-time career would have been much more difficult for my husband and me.'

ETHNICITY

Established minority ethnic groups in Europe and North America generally came from high-fertility countries at a time when fertility was falling or low in the countries where they arrived, so it is often thought that they have a much higher fertility rate than their neighbours. But to a surprising extent this is not so any longer. Two things have happened. First, fertility rates have fallen in the countries from which they have come, whether Mexico in the case of the US, Algeria in the case of France, Turkey in the case of Germany, or India and Pakistan in the case of the UK. Second, the fertility rates of immigrants tend to converge on those of their host societies. For example, Sikhs and Hindus in the UK do not have a higher fertility rate than the population as a whole and Muslim fertility rates have also fallen considerably.[12]

This phenomenon has had an impact at the national level in the US. The fertility rates of white women fell 5 per cent during the period 2006–17, and of black women 11 per cent. For women of Latin American origin, the drop was 37 per cent over more or less the same period.[13] Today, the fertility rate of Hispanic women in the US is very close to the national average.[14] This should not surprise us. More and more of the Hispanic population is second or third generation, living in low-fertility urban neighbourhoods and assimilating into them. And even for first-generation immigrants, lower fertility rates should be expected: they are leaving a very different Mexico from the country people left in the 1970s. Back then, the average Mexican woman had over four children more than US women. Today the gap is around a tenth of a child.[15]

EDUCATION

The link between increasing education and falling fertility in developing countries is clear. As women become more educated, they are more able to pursue other interests and pursuits, in particular careers, rather than simply being mothers and workers in the home and field. They are also more likely to be able to access contraception and use it successfully. Educated women are generally better able to care for their children and therefore experience lower infant mortality rates, which is a reason for having fewer children.

Bangladesh is a clear example of these trends. Between its independence from Pakistan in 1971 and today, its people have gone from mainly illiterate to overwhelmingly literate, and its infant mortality rate has fallen from about one in seven to about one in 40. During this period, its fertility rate has fallen from almost seven to barely two children per woman. And even once a country has reached the point where everyone receives around eight years of education, where just about everyone can read, and where a third or a half of each cohort goes to university, it continues to be the case that more education tends to mean fewer children. In Ghana, for example, women with no education have six children while those with 12 years of education have two. The pattern is similar in Kenya.[16] In Angola, girls with no schooling have 7.8 children, while those with tertiary education have just 2.3.[17]

In the US, meanwhile, girls leaving high school without graduating have almost 2.75 children each. Those simply leaving high school with a diploma have slightly more than two children, while those entering college but not completing a degree have slightly less than two. Those with a first degree have just 1.3. But interestingly, at the high end, there is something of an upward turn. Women with master's degrees have 1.4 children and those with PhDs have 1.5.[18] In the UK, among women born in the 1960s, those with a degree were more than twice as likely to have had no children than those without O levels (now replaced by GCSEs). Those without O levels were more than three times as likely to have had four children or more as those with a degree.[19] Among more recent cohorts, however, there is emerging evidence that the differential is narrowing, due to a rising tendency for non-educated women to have smaller families.[20]

One subtle way that education can be seen to depress fertility is through the general tendency of women to look for better-educated mates, and, some suggest, for men to look for less educated ones. This becomes a problem in societies that are sufficiently developed to offer women full opportunities in the schoolroom and university, but not advanced enough for the more educated female population to be acceptable marriage or mating material for traditionally minded men, nor for the less educated men to be acceptable marriage or mating material for the better-educated women. When we were undergraduates, a female friend of mine used to laugh at how her grandfather wished she had not gone to university. He quoted a friend of his (probably from the 1930s) whose daughter had got an education only to become an unmarriageable 'bluestocking'. We can mock such attitudes, and indeed my friend went on to become both a career woman and a wife and mother of three. (Reader, I married her.) But however uncomfortable we find it, such attitudes are still at play in much of the world.

Even in the UK, though, one frequent lament among educated women is that they cannot find a suitable man. A 2017 study of the 1970-born UK cohort showed that not having met the right partner was overwhelmingly the most common answer given by childless people who had wanted children but had not had them.[21] To some extent this has to do with a reluctance on the part of young men to commit, but it also reflects the fact that when women go to university, increasingly in larger numbers than the men of their cohort, it becomes statistically more difficult for them to 'marry up', at least from an educational perspective. (In some UK universities, there are twice as many female as male undergraduates.[22]) This is more than just anecdote. A research experiment on Tinder, a dating app, found that women in Belgium strongly selected for educated men, and were almost twice as likely to select someone with a master's than with a bachelor's degree. The men seemed more or less indifferent as to whether a woman had a master's or bachelor's degree.[23] As we shift from a world in which women are generally less educated than men to one where they are at least as educated and often more so, if we continue to hold the prejudices and preferences of a previous age it is not surprising if this messes up the patterns of partnering and mating.

It seems, therefore, that the association of education with low fertility is not just about educated women having other projects to pursue and so wanting fewer children. Indeed, there is some evidence that educated women might want *more* children than their less educated sisters; this is certainly what came out of a German study covering the period 2008–14, and it was true of men as well as women.[24] A 2011 OECD-wide survey showed almost no difference in desired fertility by educational group.[25] That people are not having the number of children they desire is a problem for us all.

POLITICS

In the US the widening cultural divide over questions of politics has been much noted in recent years – and it's a divide that even stretches to fertility rates. A county-level analysis of the 2020 election showed that strongly pro-Trump counties had a fertility rate about 25 per cent higher than pro-Biden counties, a disparity that, for a population as a whole, can make all the difference between steady-state and eventual disappearance.[26] And this may be an underestimate – the study only looked at counties with larger populations, and was therefore missing rural counties with fewer voters, which are likely to have been strongly pro-Trump and to exhibit higher fertility than the norm.

This was no flash in the pan. Comparing counties with 75 per cent plus support for Republicans with those with 75 per cent plus support for Democrats, the fertility margin in favour of the former over the latter was between 0.6 and 0.7 children per woman since 2004, after controlling for other factors like ethnicity and population density.[27] Another survey looking at completed fertility for women over 44 years of age showed that conservatives had an average of 2.5 children, versus liberals with 1.5.[28] But although this effect can be traced back to the early years of the current century, it appears not to be very much older than that. Its impact on politics has yet to be seen in full. Of course, children are no more certain to vote the way their parents did than to pray as they did, and in the US it could be with religion the same as it is with politics: the religious and the right wing have more children, but the drift in the population is towards secularism and liberalism. What is important here is not that demography is destiny, nor that a religious and conservative future is assured for the US. Rather, it is the observation that certain outlooks on life and attitudes, whether they are liked or loathed, are more probable than others to create the humans who will populate future decades.

There is some evidence that the causality runs in the opposite direction from that which we expect: to some extent it appears not just that more conservative people are more likely to have children, but that having children makes people more conservative. A study carried out over a long period in 88 countries showed that the more children that people had, the more conservative they tended to become.[29] It also appears that those who come from larger families are more conservative, at least in the US, which would tend to suggest some intergenerational retention by conservatism of its larger progeny. The greater the number of a person's siblings, the more he or she is likely to oppose gay marriage and abortion.[30]

ECONOMICS

If you talk to young couples who are not having children, or who are stopping at one, and you ask them why, many reply: 'We can't afford it.' Some 29 per cent of UK women of childbearing age say that money is holding them back from having children, and 43 per cent with at least one child declare that money concerns are preventing them from having any more. Two-thirds had delayed childbearing because they were unable to afford the costs of a newborn. For some, no doubt, it is a choice independent of economic or financial constraints, but the evidence shows, as we will see, that people want more children than they have and this suggests that something is stopping them. For many, that something is money.

This seems paradoxical for two reasons: one to do with geography, the other to do with history. Across the world, if you look at where families are largest, you find that people are poorest. The clear relationship between per capita GDP and fertility has broken down in the developed world, as we have seen, but it still holds in the developing world, and when comparing developed and developing societies. Per capita GDP in Germany, for example, is more than 100 times that in Sierra Leone, and women in the West African state are having 2.5 children more per woman than their German contemporaries.[31] Every country in the world with a fertility rate above 3.5, and almost every country with a fertility rate above 2.5, is poor. You get plenty of poor countries with low fertility rates, but don't get any rich ones with really high fertility rates.

And if we look historically as well as geographically, the same pattern occurs. As countries become richer their fertility rates fall. True, this has a lot to do with education and access to contraception, but it goes beyond that. In the UK in 1970, the pill was widespread and education through secondary level had been ubiquitous for years, yet the fertility rate was still above replacement level. Since then, income per head has doubled, so fertility has fallen, and a similar trend is true of most countries.

This is the heart of the paradox. As people get richer, they have fewer children. But they explain this by saying they are unable to afford them. And yet the voices of young people in the developed world who say that they cannot afford to start families are authentic and cannot just be brushed aside. 'People need to stop telling me to "just get on with it" if I want to have children,' says Jen Cleary, a 35-year-old former teacher in the UK. 'Most of my generation simply cannot afford to.'[32]

In the UK, two economic factors in particular are cited: the cost of childcare and the cost of housing. As far as childcare costs are concerned, it is true that these are among the highest in the OECD. Around 1.7 million women in the UK are estimated to be unable to go to work because of the cost of childcare.[33] 'Mummy, is there a baby in your tummy?' asks a four-year-old boy hoping for a sibling. 'No, there won't be any more babies,' replies his mother, who once dreamed of having three but has stopped at one.[34] Cost is the barrier in this case. 'Childcare costs are why I can't afford a second child,' confirms another mum of one.[35]

But, globally at least, this can't be the answer. In the UK, childcare costs for a two-earner family on median wages consume up to half the woman's net pay. The equivalent share in much of the world, in countries like South Korea, Italy and Germany, is a tiny fraction of this, thanks largely to government subsidies – in Germany, for example, childcare fees come to well below 5 per cent of a woman's net pay.[36] And yet the family sizes in these countries are even lower than in the UK. Something should and must be done about the costs of childcare in the UK, but don't expect a fertility miracle as a result. We haven't seen one yet in countries where childcare costs are extremely modest: fertility rates are still low – and falling.

It is a similar story with housing. In the UK, home ownership among those in their twenties fell from 50 per cent to 20 per cent in the two decades to 2013. For those in their thirties, it dropped from 70 per cent to 47 per cent over the same period. The need to rent would certainly appear to depress fertility, because of both the cost and the uncertainty.

The luxury of bringing up a family in a home you own might have seemed unimaginable to most people in, say, Victorian England, but it is a luxury to which society has become accustomed, and one that, when people are deprived of it, may well have an impact on family formation. Homes are also getting smaller, making them less well suited for large families.[37] Again, there are things that government can and should do to help, and we will come to these. However, the net effect of housing on the fertility rate is calculated to be negative but modest: a 1.3 per cent reduction in the number of births.[38] Within the UK, it is far from clear that areas with cheaper accommodation see higher fertility rates. True, ultra-expensive London has the lowest fertility rate in the country, but the fertility rate in the still-expensive south-east of England is higher than in Wales or Yorkshire, where accommodation is generally much cheaper.[39] Much of Scotland has relatively low accommodation costs, and also very low fertility rates. And looking internationally, a similar picture emerges. Accommodation is much cheaper in Germany and in Greece, for example, than in the UK, but fertility rates are lower.[40]

ANTI-NATALISM

The philosophy of anti-natalism is too obscure, too little known about and too little understood to be having a direct impact on birth rates yet. But this pernicious and misanthropic way of thinking, often driven by worries about the climate, is working its way into the behaviour and potentially the fertility choices of the young generation that is now coming to parenthood age. 'I wanted to have a child, but I was also looking at the planet and thinking: "Well, what kind of future will we have if there's more of the same?"'[41] Some 96 per cent of people surveyed said they were worried about climate change for potential future offspring.[42]

There are two aspects to the environmental anti-natalism argument: first, every extra child is an extra emitter, which drives the climate catastrophe onward. Second, given the supposedly dire outlook for humankind, it is unfair to bring a child into a world that's going to a globally warmed hell in a handcart. Both perspectives are promoted by celebrities. The Duke and Duchess of Sussex, for example, publicly stated that they did not intend to have a third child (unlike their in-laws the Prince and Princess of Wales) because of climate change.[43] Rising US Democrat star Alexandria Ocasio-Cortez insists, 'It is basically a scientific consensus that the lives of our children are going to be very difficult. And it does lead, I think, young people to have a legitimate question: is it OK to still have children?'[44] Analysts at bank Morgan Stanley believe that climate concerns are now a major factor in falling fertility rates.[45]

The Birthstrike Movement's website says it all:

> Are you terrified about the future that lies ahead for contemporary and future youth? Do you want to maximise your positive impact on the Climate Change Crisis? Are you tired of leaders ignoring the needs of humanity and perpetuating a constant state of consumption and destruction? You can

protect children while fighting climate change and systematic corruption by refusing to procreate![46]

And some do. A UK-based journalist called Holly Brockwell campaigned hard for the right to get herself sterilised from the tender age of 26, and eventually she succeeded. 'Every year for the last four years my GP has refused my decision,' she complained. 'I couldn't even get a referral. The response was always: "You're far too young to take such a drastic decision."' Ms Brockwell clearly thinks she is being public-minded: 'It's cheaper than actually having a child on the NHS, it's cheaper than having IVF and all sorts of other things that the NHS offers.'

She added: 'In the long term it will save them money. The "lifestyle choice" argument is a silly one to me, because having children is a lifestyle choice. Both should be equally respected, surely? Why is one more OK than the other?'[47] Another woman sterilised at 27 lamented: 'Having children is selfish. Every person who is born uses more food, more water, more land, more fossil fuels, more trees, and produces more rubbish, more pollution, more greenhouse gases, and adds to the problem of overpopulation.'[48] We will examine these arguments more closely in Chapter 6.

In summary, then, a number of distinct factors are coming together and resulting in fertility rates plunging across the world. Much of the world is completing its fertility transition. People in Asia, Africa and Latin America are getting richer and more educated, assimilating the fact that they are likely to lose far fewer children in infancy than did their parents' generation, and taking control of their own fertility. This is something we should welcome.

But in the developed world, and even in some still quite poor countries, we are significantly undershooting replacement-level fertility and building in population decline. As people become more liberal and more secular their fertility falls. In some societies generally low birth rates are being partially offset by the more religious and conservative, but it seems paradoxical to say that the key driver is unaffordability when poorer societies in the past have had higher fertility rates than those of today and given that it is the poorest countries in today's world who still have the most children.

SOUTH KOREA: THE PERFECT STORM

In the early summer of 2023, I found myself in South Korea, giving a talk on the subject of demography. My last two books have been translated into Korean (there are plans for this one too) and population matters are a hot topic in the country. It is not surprising: at around 0.8 children per woman, South Korea has the lowest fertility rate of any country in the world. After my talk I took a trip to a rural hotel attractive to families. I noticed at breakfast a great crowd of grandparents, parents and children. What was almost entirely missing was siblings. The children appeared overwhelmingly to be without brothers or sisters.

A fertility rate of 0.8 per woman means in principle that two people in one cohort become 0.8 of a person in the next. One hundred grandparents will produce 40 children, who will in turn create 16 grandchildren. In two generations, 84 per cent of the population will have disappeared. In fact, things are slightly worse for Korea – as fertility rates are always expressed per *woman*. The problem in South Korea is that today's cohort of childbearing-age people is disproportionately *male* as a result of son-preference selective abortions a generation ago when ultrasound technology became available. In some places, there were more than 125 males born for every 100 females.[49] If fertility rates are measured *per woman*, and if women are less than half of the cohort, then in reality the population is diminishing even faster, as each woman needs to have more children to make up the difference.

Korea in some ways represents a perfect storm, a combination of many of the factors we have mentioned above. It is a very urban country, with half the population living in the greater Seoul area, and most of the rest in large cities.[50] It is a wealthy country, where GDP per capita has soared in the past half-century and is now close to Japan's, whereas as recently as the 1990s it was less than one-third of the level.[51] South Koreans are also highly educated, with more than 70 per cent of each year group enrolling in university.[52] Recognised as one of the world's most competitive societies, South Korea is an extreme example of urban, wealthy people investing more and more in fewer and fewer children. If your highest priority is getting your child into the best university, and this requires much parental input of time and money, it may make sense to have just the one child and devote all resources to him or her.

As well as being very status-conscious and competitive, Korea is in many ways traditional when it comes to issues of gender, and it is likely that the problem of hypergamy – whereby women look for more educated men and men avoid more educated women – is common. South Korea is precisely the 'caught in the middle' sort of society where fertility tends to be low: on the one hand, women are given great educational opportunities, but on the other they are expected to conform with traditional lifestyles. Women in Korea do 80 per cent of the household chores, and men just 20 per cent.[53] The traditional social attitudes in Korea are also seen by the very low share of births outside wedlock: just a few percentage points, as against close to half in the OECD as a whole.[54] The number of marriages in South Korea has more than halved since the mid-1990s: if far fewer people are getting married and almost nobody is having children outside wedlock, the birth rate is almost bound to plummet. On the whole, developed countries with high levels of education and income but low levels of extramarital fertility have very low total fertility. And Koreans are finding it harder to develop the kind of relationships which will lead to marriage: a recent study showed that 43 per cent of women and 29 per cent of men in Seoul had not had sex during the past year.[55]

Two other factors seem to be feeding into making South Korea such a low-fertility country. One is the lack of an Abrahamic religious background, which, as we have seen, can help prop up fertility rates. Although most of those with a religion in Korea are Christian, this is a relatively recent phenomenon, meaning that the cultural correlates of Christianity don't apply. And most of the society has no religion at all.[56] The second is the prevalence of a fairly anti-natal culture. Hundreds of restaurants, cafes, museums and other public places have signs insisting 'No Children, No Pets'.[57] When that is the attitude at the level of the institution, it is not surprising that 'no children' is what we see at the level of the nation.

4

WHERE FERTILITY PERSISTS

I N this chapter, we will look for indications from elsewhere that rising levels of income, education and urbanisation need not lead inexorably to sub-replacement fertility rates. First we will take a look at those places where economic and social development are well underway but where we have not seen a collapse in fertility rates, particularly focusing on Indonesia. Then we will take a look at Israel, the only fully developed country with advanced-world levels of income, education and urbanisation where nevertheless people are having enough children to replace themselves, and by some margin.

INDONESIA:
THE GOLDILOCKS SCENARIO

Several years ago, I found myself working in Jakarta, the steamy, polluted, maddening but exhilarating capital of Indonesia. With more than 10 million people, Jakarta is the largest city in a country of more than a quarter of a billion inhabitants, the world's fourth most populous state. Jakarta is a place that throbs with life and, in many ways, it is typical of large cities in the developing world. Its pavements are narrow and often broken; housing is frequently shabby and makeshift; and its infrastructure creaks, manifested by congested roads and regular flooding. The contrast with relatively nearby Singapore, for example, could hardly be greater. But neither is Jakarta the kind of massive shanty town I learned about in school geography classes in the 1970s, when we were told of third-world megalopolises full of hunger and despair, with people living in unthinkably horrible conditions on the edge of survival, but joined every day by newcomers from even more desperate villages in the hinterland. Instead, Jakarta today is a city somewhere between what we traditionally think of as the developed and the developing world, transitioning from what we used to think of as a typical third-world city to something more like a city in Europe, North America or East Asia. For anyone interested in global change, that is part of its thrill.

I once decided to walk the fairly short distance from our hotel to the office rather than travel by cab as normal. My colleagues told me I would regret it – and they were right. Apart from the dreadful air quality, crossing the road in many places was rendered near impossible by the seemingly endless flow of motorbikes, usually driven by young men, often with a young woman at the back. Sometimes the young women were in the front seat. In any case, navigating the crossings made the experience exhausting, asphyxiating and even slower than by car.

The most striking thing about Jakarta is its youth. You see it on its pavements, in its street markets and in the growing number of air-conditioned malls that now dot the city. Again, this is something transitional. It is not like the dusty Kolkata

I encountered on my travels in India in the 1980s, nor is it the dreary Bamako I remember from my time in Mali in the 1990s, both full of malnourished small children. Those cities at that time had the disturbing and dystopic qualities of a vast undernourished kindergarten. But neither is Jakarta like the towns in northern Spain I have visited in recent years, where almost everyone is elderly, where most people seem to be sitting sipping coffee in the sun, and where all the youngsters have vanished. Rather, it falls somewhere in between. It is a city of people mainly in their twenties, hassling and hustling and trying to get ahead. Jakarta (and indeed Indonesia more generally) has the energy of a place enjoying a classic demographic dividend. How did it get there, and what comes next?

What makes Indonesia of interest to demographers is the fact that it has a fertility rate of between two and three, and it has retained this for a considerable period of time. This is an ideal zone, a Goldilocks scenario: not too hot, not too cold, not too high, and not too low. If the rest of us are going to thrive, we have to learn something from countries like Indonesia.

Having declared its independence in the wake of Japan's 1945 defeat at the end of the Second World War, and having resisted the reimposition of Dutch colonial rule, the South East Asian archipelago nation was led in its early decades by President Sukarno. A founder of the Non-Aligned Movement, with anti-Western leanings and a degree of support from local communists, Sukarno was overthrown in a bloody military coup by General Suharto in 1965. Suharto ruthlessly crushed the communists, killing at least 400,000 people.[1]

At that stage Indonesia was failing not only politically but economically and developmentally too. And it had the demography to match: fertility rates of between five and six children per woman, life expectancy at around 55 and an infant mortality rate of more than one in ten. There were plenty of poorer and more desperate countries in the world, but given its rich endowments, Indonesia at that point was turning out to be something of a disappointment.

But progress since then has been steady and sustained, particularly since Suharto's fall in 1998 and the subsequent emergence of a more stable democratic order. Income per capita has increased six- or sevenfold since the early 1970s.[2] Infant mortality rates have fallen by 80 per cent, and life expectancy has extended to the early seventies, close to the worst-performing US states like West Virginia, or to the life expectancy of men in Glasgow, Scotland, or to Russia as a whole.

Indonesia is a textbook case of economic and human development, reflected powerfully in the demographic data. The illiteracy rate was halved between 1970 and 2000, and today adult inability to read has more or less been banished altogether.[3] The share of those with university degrees, although still quite low at 17.9 per cent, is rising.[4] The proportion of the population living in towns has risen in the past 50 years from under a fifth to over a half.[5]

Indonesia's measurable advances in income, urbanisation and education are the classic hallmarks of the changes that accompany moving through the demographic transition. Back in the late 1960s and early 1970s, Indonesian women were having five or six children each. As the country developed, urbanised and grew more educated, so the fertility rate came down. Sukarno had pursued a policy of pro-natalism (or, given the high level, we might say hyper-natalism), attempting to deal with local overpopulation by encouraging those from the most densely populated areas to move to remoter parts.[6]

(This could be seen as the demographic arm of the policy of 'Javanisation', spreading the culture of Indonesia's most populous island.)

Under Suharto this policy was reversed and the National Family Planning Coordinating Body was established in 1970. Within just five years a third of married women in their fertile years were reached by the programme, and by the early 1990s, the fertility rate of Indonesia had fallen below three.[7] While this all went hand in hand with social and economic development, it was also underpinned by consistent government action, starting in the 1960s in the two most densely populated islands, Java and Bali, with the establishment of fieldworkers, targets, incentives and enhanced data collection.[8]

But once it reached this level, the decline in fertility slowed, and it has had three decades in the Goldilocks zone with a total fertility rate of two to three. (Thailand, for example, reached a total fertility rate of three a decade or so earlier than Indonesia, in the early 1980s, but by the early 1990s its fertility rate had collapsed to below replacement level, where it has stayed ever since, at a painfully low 1.3.) In 2065, Indonesia is projected by the UN to have more than three people of working age to support every person above age 65. Ageing will be gradual and therefore should be manageable. Thailand's dependency ratio by 2065, on the other hand, will be twice the level in Indonesia, or three working-age people to support two retired people. By then the median Thai will be more than a whole decade older than the median Indonesian. As soon as mid-century, just a generation away, the dependency ratio in Thailand will be as bad as it is now in Japan, and from then on things will just keep getting worse. And Thailand will not have the wealth or capital of today's Japan to obviate the hardest effects of ageing.

Already we can see the impact of these different demographic paths. Indonesia's economic growth has outstripped Thailand's in recent decades. Between 2000 and 2019, Indonesia's economy consistently grew at around 5 per cent while Thailand's, apart from being much less consistent, underperformed that level for most of the time.[9] And if demography is anything to go by, Indonesia has decades more of outperformance ahead of it. At present, the average Thai is half as rich again as the average Indonesian.[10] But the gap is narrowing. By the middle of this century, the countries will be very different. Thailand will be ageing, sagging and indebted; Indonesia will have at the very least some fuel in the tank. And demography will be at the root of it.

REAPING THE DEMOGRAPHIC DIVIDEND

At the stage in the demographic transition when people are starting to have smaller families, but before there is significant ageing or population decline, the economy often does very well. At this stage the fertility rate is normally between two and three, there are plenty of young people entering the workforce and they are having smaller and later families than the very early and very large families their parents had. There are broadly two explanations for this. One puts demography in the driving seat. It suggests that people in a plentiful workforce, the product of high fertility two or three decades previously but now unencumbered by their own large broods of children, are free to participate in the labour market with potentially highly stimulating effects. The other explanation is that demography is the outcome of other positive developments: education, urbanisation and rising incomes, so it is hardly surprising that a large cohort of young adults accompanied by a drop in the fertility rate is associated with economic dynamism.

Whatever it is that gets the process started in the first place, there are two further advantages of this kind of demographic scenario. First, with smaller families, more can be invested in the children who are born, which means they are better trained and educated when they enter the workforce, so they can go on to be highly productive themselves. Second, the young workforce will be saving for its retirement, creating domestically generated capital for investment and building the country's capital base.

Japan went through its era of spectacular economic growth from the 1950s to the 1980s, when its working-age population was high. It started to go into relative decline and stagnation precisely as its workforce peaked. South Korea's economic glory years were likewise in the period when buoyant numbers of people were entering the workforce and the fertility rate was falling. The same is true of Taiwan. Mainland China enjoyed its extraordinary and world-changing industrialisation and growth in the decades following a sharp fall in its birth rate. (As noted earlier, this decline in fertility would have happened without the egregious one-child policy, albeit perhaps more slowly.) And as we have seen, Indonesia has thrived as its fertility rate has gently fallen and its young working-age population has boomed.

But the right demographic alignment is no guarantee of economic success. There are sadly plenty of cases where a decade or two after fertility rates have moved into the two-to-three-children-per-woman zone, things stopped looking as rosy as they have done recently in Indonesia. The most obvious case is Syria. It was heading rapidly downwards towards a total fertility rate of three when revolution and civil war broke out in 2010. At that point the fertility rate was at 3.4 and had fallen by two children over the course of the two preceding decades. But even before the war broke out, there was no indication that Syria was heading towards anything like a demographic dividend and economic take-off. Instead, the country continued to labour under the burden of its oppressive and corrupt regime. Since then, Syria has come apart. Likewise, Lebanon is a failed state despite having a large cohort of twenty- and thirty-somethings and a now much moderated fertility rate. Again, political instability is a critical component of this failure, just as democracy and political stability were crucial to Indonesia's success. It is clear that the right demographic situation may be a necessary condition of economic success: it is hard to imagine a country with a fertility rate above four really thriving in the modern world. But it is not a sufficient one. The right demography alone cannot deliver a dividend.

One key component, of course, is political. It is difficult to take advantage of any underlying social trends if you are ruled over by a kleptocracy or are experiencing extreme political instability. Education clearly matters as well: an inflow of young workers much more educated than the cohorts already in the workforce creates a powerful tonic. But without the sheer heft of a new emerging generation, sizeable enough to make an impact, the demographic dividend cannot be achieved.[11]

Of course, you cannot enjoy the demographic dividend forever. Part of the dividend is the slowing down of fertility so that the new generation, of both sexes, can make its contribution to the economy and to the development of the nation without the encumbrance of half a dozen children per woman. Once past that point, though, if you are able to maintain a stable fertility rate of two to three children per woman for several decades, as Indonesia has, the effects of the dividend will not dissipate as rapidly as we are seeing in Thailand, a classic case of a country likely to get old before it gets rich.

GOLDILOCKS FOR HOW LONG?

As noted above, Indonesia is now heading towards fertility replacement level after three decades in the zone just above it. Where it will go from here is hard to predict. In a decade or two we might be looking at an Indonesia where childbearing is as rare as in Thailand or Japan. But Indonesia will have had the advantage of fertility falling later and will therefore have longer to prepare for the ultimate shrinking of the workforce and population. The United Nations Population Division, which produces the most authoritative projections, suggests that the fertility rate in Indonesia will drift downwards only slowly between now and the end of the century, from today's near-replacement rate of 2.2 towards about 1.8. If that happened, it would be a fairly smooth landing compared to what much of the world will experience.

One indication of where fertility rates are heading is the number of children that people say they want. In Indonesia, the share wanting two is around 40 per cent, with another 40 per cent saying they want more than two, and only very few saying they want one or none. Some 20 per cent of respondents, rather than giving a particular number, declare that they are leaving it up to God.[12] This does not suggest a society in which fertility rates are on the verge of crashing towards north-east Asian or European levels.

One factor does appear to be Islam, the religion of the overwhelming majority of Indonesians. Fertility rates in East and South East Asia have fallen earliest and fastest where Buddhism prevails or has historically prevailed (in Japan, China and Thailand, for example) and less quickly in societies that are predominantly Muslim or Christian (like Indonesia and the Philippines). Neighbouring Malaysia, culturally and linguistically similar to Indonesia, though with large Chinese Buddhist and Indian Hindu minorities, has a fertility rate well below replacement level today. But the evidence from Albania (total fertility rate 1.4) and Iran (total fertility rate 1.7) is that Islam is no absolute guarantee in this respect, so the preponderance of Muslims does not necessarily mean that Indonesia will avoid a low fertility future.

Additionally, there are still many Indonesian women who live in remote areas, have only modest levels of education and do not have easy access to contraception. This suggests that the current fertility rate does not yet fully reflect women's choices.[13] Once these women too have complete control over their fertility, we might expect fertility rates to fall further. Indonesia's Goldilocks days may be numbered.

INDIA AND THE GOLDILOCKS SCENARIO

At some point in early 2023, India overtook China as the world's most populous country. We cannot be sure exactly when this event took place: the putative date is a function of population projections and we'd need to have a God's-eye view to know precisely when a death north of the Himalayas, or a birth to the south, caused the crossover to occur. Both countries are immense, and their record-keeping is imperfect. Still, we do know that, for the first time in millennia, China has ceased to be the world's most populous state. If India had not been partitioned in 1947, and still included the territories of the modern states of Pakistan and Bangladesh, this would have happened some time ago.

In some ways, the demographic parallels between India and China mirror those between Indonesia and Thailand. China and Thailand developed more quickly and earlier from an economic and industrial perspective, underwent extremely fast declines in their fertility, cashed in on their demographic dividend early, and now face falling or at least stagnant populations. India and Indonesia have developed more slowly, and wherever fertility rates go in the coming years, they have demographic momentum built in, and have years or even decades of demographic dividend ahead of them.

But even though India and Indonesia today have a similar fertility rate, at a little above two, there is an important difference. Whereas Indonesia's fertility rate has experienced a fairly long period of stability, India's has been falling continuously. And, critically, India has arrived at replacement fertility while its per capita GDP is half that of Indonesia's and its population is less well educated and considerably less urban.[14] This suggests that India is inherently less pro-natal than Indonesia, which is in line with what we would expect from a predominantly Hindu nation as opposed to a predominantly Muslim one, given the fact that Abrahamic religions tend to delay the fertility collapse. Indeed, the difference in fertility rates by religion in India, although not as pronounced as some Hindu nationalists claim, is about half a child in favour of Muslims, backing up the association of Abrahamic religion with higher fertility.[15] While increases in development lead to falls in fertility, the presence of a pro-natal religion tends to slow this down.

Wealthier Indians seem to express the same existential angst that is holding back childbearing in the West, despite much stronger pressure from the older generation.[16] Parental pressure to have grandchildren remains, but as the generations move on, that too will fade. It was once a noted feature of Chinese family life, with its tradition of ancestor worship, but China has not maintained its birth rate even in the absence of coercive anti-natalism.

The other reason to expect that India will not experience a Goldilocks scenario is that much of the country has already plunged into sub-replacement territory. In Indonesia most of the regions are more or less at replacement level, with a few more remote ones significantly above it (such as West Papua in New Guinea).[17] In India too, some of the more remote and less developed regions have high fertility (such as Meghalaya in the north-east), but these are small. While the still relatively poor Hindi belt in the north (Uttar Pradesh and Bihar) has fertility rates above replacement, the richer and more developed states have seen family sizes decline in the last decade or so. In West Bengal fertility has halved since the early 1990s, and is now at Japanese levels. All the states of the south – Kerala, Andhra Pradesh, Karnataka and Tamil Nadu – now have fertility rates close to the UK's.[18] Literacy in some places may be near universal and urbanisation rising, but for fertility to have fallen to Japanese and UK levels in places where income is only a fraction of that in the developed world suggests an absence of the kind of moderate pro-natalism needed to keep India as a whole in the Goldilocks zone for long.

Like China, India is too poor to attract large-scale immigration, and is likely still to be so when historic low fertility hits the size of its workforce and starts to be seen in its dependency ratio. And again, like China, India's population is too large for immigration on anything other than a gargantuan scale to make any material difference. But as well as ongoing movement from the countryside to the towns, India is also experiencing internal migration from less developed, high-fertility states, predominantly in the north, to more developed, low-fertility ones in the south. Tamil Nadu, the largest state in the south, with a fertility rate of just 1.4, has around 3.5 million workers from other parts of the country.[19] Like Europe and North America, these states have the advantage of a hinterland from which they can attract migration – in their case, within the borders of the same country – but given the pace with which fertility is falling in northern India (down a whole child in Bihar and a child and a half in Uttar Pradesh in 15 years) they cannot expect it to last forever.[20]

THE OTHER GOLDILOCKSES

Worryingly, with one exception – which we will examine later in this chapter – all the countries that might be considered 'developed' have fertility rates below replacement level. While Indonesia and India have fertility at or just above replacement level, they are still quite poor, and as they become more developed the concern is that they too will slip below that level. The countries on the continent of Africa with fertility rates of two to three, whether north of the Sahara or in the south of the continent, are still fairly poor. None of these countries has proven that it can resist the low-fertility siren calls that come with modernity. All that they have shown to date is that their fertility rates have not fallen below replacement level before they can be considered wealthy, urbanised and educated. Even though the two countries have a similar level of economic development, South Africa, with a total fertility rate of 2.4, is in a better position demographically than Jamaica, with a total fertility rate of 1.4; but there is as yet no guarantee that South Africa will retain this level as it develops further.

Beyond Indonesia and Africa's northern and southern fringes, the general pattern is for countries earlier and earlier in their progress towards development to experience fast-falling fertility and a descent to below replacement level rather than remaining for long in the Goldilocks zone. In Central Asia there are a number of countries where the unusual post-Soviet conditions depressed fertility but from which it has bounced back towards and even beyond three children per woman. Argentina is too an exception, having held its fertility rate at between two and three from the early 1990s until quite recently. Once seen as a country of great promise, Argentina has failed both economically and politically, and now has a per capita income not much above Cuba's at Power Purchasing Parity. Yet it is a relatively educated and urban country. Fertility rates in Argentina may now be coming down below two, with some sources suggesting that it nosedived to 1.5 during the Covid crisis. It seems that Argentina has in very recent years followed the pattern seen elsewhere, of low fertility that starts among the most educated and highest echelons of society, and then works its way downwards.[21] But the long period during which its fertility rate was between two and three puts Argentina in a reasonably good position demographically for the next few decades at least.

About 90 per cent of Argentinians identify as Catholic, and Argentina is the homeland of Pope Francis, who has made pro-natalism an important part of his message. 'Today... we see a form of selfishness,' he told an audience in 2022.

> We see that some people do not want to have a child. Sometimes they have one, and that's it, but they have dogs and cats that take the place of children. This may make people laugh, but it is a reality... [This] is a denial of fatherhood and motherhood and diminishes us, takes away our humanity.[22]

Asked by a woman to bless what he thought was a baby, the Pope found out it was in fact a canine rather than a human for whom his benediction was being sought. 'I lost my patience and told her off: there are many children who are hungry, and you bring me a dog?'[23]

But the words of Pope Francis could well be addressed to his countrymen as much as to any others. Fewer than 20 per cent of Argentinians are actively involved in the religion.[24] And as we have seen, traditionally Catholic countries in Europe like Spain and Italy have some of the continent's, and the world's, lowest fertility rates. Argentinian governments have not espoused pro-natalism, and efforts continued during the 2010s to reduce teenage pregnancy.[25] Argentina was only the third Latin American country fully to legalise abortion. It seems, therefore, that the country's Goldilocks period was more a function of the Catholic Church holding back the tide than any real pro-natalism on the part of the Pope's compatriots.

Another apparent Goldilocks has been Sri Lanka, slightly surprising given the country's approximately 70 per cent Buddhist population. Sri Lanka's total fertility rate has been between two and three since the mid-1980s, and has been around or just above two since the start of this century. Fertility rates here, as elsewhere in Asia, are clearly higher among Muslims than among Hindus or Buddhists.[26] Although strictly below replacement level, two is enough to ensure something close to a stable population where infant and childhood mortality have been radically reduced. (Sri Lankan infant mortality is not much higher than that of the US, an extraordinary achievement for a still relatively poor country.) But although the use of contraceptives is widespread, there was still judged to be unmet need as recently as 2015, when fertility rates were already very close to two.[27]

Indonesia and Argentina may be more inherently pro-natal than some of their neighbours, resisting the sharp plunges into sub-replacement territory seen by countries like Korea, Cuba or Thailand. (Cuba, for example, spent a grand total of four years in the mid-1970s in the Goldilocks zone before falling below it by the end of that decade and staying there ever since.) However, as we have seen, in many cases those dwelling in the Goldilocks zone appear to be in the process of falling out of it. The tide seems to have been held back by a now-waning commitment to Abrahamic religions, a lack of full access to family planning and relative poverty. These countries' extended periods of reasonably healthy fertility rates will partially but not fully shield them from the sharpest demographic challenges faced by others. As they become more secular and wealthier, and as the traditional measures preventing women from fully controlling their own fertility are removed, they risk falling into the same sub-replacement zone as the rest of us.

To find a model for humanity seeking a sustainable level of fertility, we have to look to a country that has managed this despite high levels of urbanisation, education and income, and where, despite the fact that women can control their own fertility, they are still choosing to have two or three children on average. There is only one such country on the planet.

THE ISRAELI EXCEPTION

In the spring of 2023, I found myself visiting the maternity ward of a large Israeli hospital in a township outside Tel Aviv. Unlike such facilities in much of the developed world, it was a hive of activity. Russian-speaking midwives were bustling in and out of delivery suites, while Ethiopian families waited patiently for their newborns to be checked. In similar places across Israel, you will find Muslim women doctors in head-scarves providing advice to bewigged ultra-Orthodox mothers of European origin, as their bearded and black-hatted husbands look on. Jews of Iraqi, Yemeni and Moroccan origin come and go with babies in their arms, as excited Arab siblings greet tiny newly arrived brothers and sisters. In many ways its maternity wards are a microcosm of Israel, not only in the ethnic and religious diversity hard to find anywhere else in the Middle East, but also in its young and fertile population, which is unique among comparably developed countries.

What makes this tiny country on the south-eastern shore of the Mediterranean of interest to demographers is not its high fertility per se: at three children per woman, Israelis have only half the number of children borne by women in the highest-fertility states like Chad or the Central African Republic. Rather, it is the fact that Israel is a modern, dynamic and successful country that is fully part of the developed world, where women have a fertility rate well above replacement level and a whole child more than in any other country at a similar level of development. And this is a fertility rate that has risen, from 2.5 to three over the past generation, while that of so much of the rest of the world has slumped. Very recent data suggest a slight fall in Israeli fertility, but it is too small and too recent for us to draw any significant conclusions from it: Israeli fertility remains exceptionally high.[28]

The basic data speak for themselves. Per capita income in Israel is higher than in countries including Italy, Germany and the UK.[29] Its share of population with a university degree (close to 50 per cent) almost exactly matches the OECD average, below countries like Korea and the US but above others like Italy and Austria.[30] It ranks ahead of Ireland and Italy in patents submitted relative to its population.[31] It is as urbanised as the Netherlands and more urbanised than Denmark.[32] Israel does not have high fertility because it is still progressing through the first demographic transition, but because it has somehow invented or discovered the demographic elixir of life: how to be a fully developed country without getting itself into a demographic death spiral.

Israeli women not only have three to four times as many children as their no richer, no more educated and no more urban peers in South Korea, but they have more than twice as many babies as women in significantly less developed countries, such as Thailand and Jamaica. As recently as the mid-1980s, Iranians had almost four children more than Israelis; now they have more than a child less. By the normal correlates associated with falling and low fertility – high levels of income, education and urbanisation – we should expect Israel to be part of the ever-larger pack which, having passed through its demographic transition, has a fertility rate of between one and two. The fact that Israel is so far removed from this suggests that something interesting is going on. If the world is to stave off the impending demographic winter, it might have something to learn from a nation that takes seriously the words of Deuteronomy 30:19: 'Choose life, that you and your descendants may live.'

THE EMERGING ISRAELI ANOMALY

Although there have been Jews living in what is now Israel for millennia, it was only with the Zionist movement founded by Theodor Herzl in the late nineteenth century that mass immigration of Jews began and the Jewish presence grew exponentially. It was driven partly by a religious and ideological attachment to the Land of Israel, but more forcefully by the wave of persecutions driving Jews from their homes in Europe and culminating in the Holocaust. From the early 1920s immigration was more or less open to Jews under the terms of the Balfour Declaration, Britain's public statement in favour of the creation of a national homeland for the Jews in Palestine, enshrined in the League of Nations mandate. But Arab opposition to that immigration and Britain's eagerness to appease Arab sentiments meant a closing of the gates on the eve of the Second World War, when European Jewry was most desperate to find an escape from Nazi persecution and genocide. Nevertheless, by 1946, the country had more than

600,000 Jewish inhabitants, constituting about a third of the total population.[33]

The Jewish population of the 'Yishuv', the Jewish community in pre-independence Israel, was overwhelmingly made up of Jews of European extraction. There are two reasons for this. First, before the Holocaust, European or Ashkenazi Jews were the predominant element in world Jewry, making up around 90 per cent of the total following the nineteenth-century population explosion in their communities.[34] Second, as a modern nationalist movement, Zionism had more immediate appeal to the Jews of eastern and central Europe than it had to more traditional and static communities in the Middle East and North Africa, whom modernity was only starting to touch. The traditional Sephardi communities in Jerusalem and some other cities were relatively small in number, as were those from Yemen who had arrived over the preceding decades in response to local persecution.

The predominantly Ashkenazi population had to a large extent passed through its demographic transition. High birth rates and falling mortality with the advent of modernity had led to a Jewish population explosion in Russia, Poland and Ukraine in the nineteenth century, but by the mid-twentieth century, low fertility had taken root. Although fertility data for this period are not available, the crude birth rate of the Jews in Mandate Palestine suggests a level similar to that in Europe at the time, much lower than that of the Palestinian Arabs.[35] Jewish population growth at that point depended on immigration rather than fertility.

In Israel's first five years of independence, it received around 700,000 immigrants, more or less doubling its Jewish population. The first wave was made up of European Jews from detention camps, Holocaust survivors and displaced people, many motivated to move to the Jewish state by their harrowing experiences during the Second World War. After the War of Independence, from 1949, huge waves of Jews arrived from the predominantly Muslim countries of the Middle East, largely driven by persecution and expropriation in countries such as Egypt, Iraq and Libya. The historic Jewish communities in these countries, many preceding the arrival of Islam by centuries, were reduced from tens or hundreds of thousands to a small handful, or to nothing, within decades. Many of these immigrants came from countries far from fully through their demographic transition, and they brought with them a high fertility rate – about six or seven children per woman compared with two to 2.5 for Israeli Jews of European origin.[36] But their arrival in Israel, where they soon made up half the Jewish population, came with a rapid process of modernisation and a concomitant fall in fertility, and the fertility rates of the new arrivals from the Middle East and North Africa converged towards those of their co-religionists of European origin, with whom they intermingled and increasingly intermarried.

At the same time, the very high fertility rate of Israeli Arabs, who today make up a fifth of the population of Israel (excluding the West Bank and Gaza), began to fall thanks to the same processes of modernisation. For the country as a whole this meant a sharp reduction in fertility, as the total fertility rate of around four in 1960 fell to a little over 2.5 by 1990.

The Israeli government was keen to ensure a Jewish majority and certainly promoted childbearing, although as a democratic state it felt it could not do so on a discriminatory basis. Founding prime minister David Ben-Gurion was deeply interested in and arguably obsessed by demography. 'If for the time being we could count on two million more to give us a total Jewish population of four and a half million, then I would no longer fear for Israel's fate,' he maintained. A later prime minister, Levi Eshkol, expressed a similar sentiment: 'The starting point is that this is our only place in the world. In some place, in this place, we have to stop being a minority.'[37] The main focus, to ensure that the Jewish population of the country remained a majority, was on 'aliya' or immigration, initially largely from the Islamic world, but increasingly from the 1970s onwards, and particularly in the 1990s, from the Soviet Union and its successor states.[38]

So far, so largely normal, as far as fertility is concerned. A process of modernisation, with the ubiquitous trio of urbanisation, education and rising incomes, brought the whole population to the socio-economic condition of its most advanced element, and fertility overall fell towards replacement level. All that was unusual in the Israeli case, although hardly unique, was the different starting points of the various communities. But from the mid-1990s, something strange started to happen. Instead of Israeli fertility sinking towards two children per woman and then below it, it started gradually and steadily to rise, reaching about three by 2010, and staying at or around that level ever since. What is particularly surprising about this is that it occurred as Israel was absorbing a huge influx of Jews from the former Soviet Union, a low-fertility population from a low-fertility country. On arrival in Israel, the fertility rate of Russian Jews seemed almost miraculously to rise towards the local norm, two and a half times the level of the Russian Jews who remained in Russia.[39]

AN ANATOMY OF ISRAELI FERTILITY

To understand what is happening in Israel with regard to fertility rates, we need to understand the differences between the various sections of society.

The first thing to observe about Israel is that the fertility rate is very highly correlated with religiosity, at least among the Jewish four-fifths of the population. Women defined as ultra-Orthodox have 6.4 children each today, a rate higher than that of any country other than Niger.[40] There is evidence that this rate is falling, but not by much, nor very fast. Twenty years ago, the number was about seven. This will come as no surprise to the casual observer who travels around Israel. It is easy to know when you are in an ultra-Orthodox or Haredi area from the appearance of its residents, with the men in black suits and black hats sporting beards and long ringlets, the women dressed modestly, their heads covered by wigs, and above all children everywhere. Modi'in Illit, a small town on the borders of pre-1967 Israel and the West Bank, is a good illustration. In 2019 it had nearly 44,000 inhabitants aged under 14, and fewer than 700 aged over 65.[41] In Germany, a country with an old and fast-ageing population, there are more than two over-65s for every one child under 15. In Modi'in Illit, there are more than 60 under-15s for every senior citizen over 65.

Although the Haredim are clearly growing quickly, they still make up only 13 per cent of the country's population, so even their astronomic fertility rate cannot tell the whole story. And it does not. Those Israeli Jews who are categorised as 'religious' but not Haredi have consistently experienced a fertility rate of around four children per woman. This may not put them quite on par with the highest-fertility countries in Africa, but it does mean that they have about twice as many children as women in India, for example.

You can see this also on the streets in areas like Giv'at Shmuel near Tel Aviv, an area with a population that could be described as 'modern Orthodox', where children may not be quite as numerous as in Modi'in Illit or nearby Haredi B'nei Barak, but where nevertheless their predominance in the population is very evident. The age balance here is less striking but still significant. Unlike Germany's more than two over-65s to every person under 15, there are two under-15s to every person over 65.[42] Among those who describe themselves as 'traditional', the fertility rate is around three, and even the most secular portion of the population just about manages to replace itself, with a fertility rate of two.[43] It is noteworthy that even when you strip out Israel's religious and Arab citizens and those with some religious affiliation, and pare back to the most secular element in society, it still has a fertility rate higher than that of any other developed country.

As for the fifth of Israelis who are not Jewish, as recently as the 1960s, the Arab-Palestinian community within Israel had a phenomenal fertility rate of nine children per woman.[44] What has happened among this population is a simpler and more classic decline in fertility, as it has become richer, more educated and more urban. Life expectancy and infant mortality rates among Israeli Arabs, for example, are at around US levels, so it is hardly surprising that they no longer have an extremely elevated fertility rate.[45] But here too, religion makes a difference. Israeli Muslims have a fertility rate of around three children per woman, very close to the overall Jewish rate, while Christians and Druze have fertility rates of slightly less than two.[46]

Compared with religion, other drivers of fertility in Israel are less pronounced but still worth considering. There is some evidence that, controlling for religious observance and intensity, Israel has the same left/right fertility differential as observed in the US. Just as Trump voters have more children than Biden voters, so right-wing nationalists in Israel seem to have about 35 per cent more children than their more left-leaning fellow citizens.[47] Israel's settler population of Jews who live in the West Bank, an area under Israeli control since the Six Day War in 1967, constitutes a mixed group, including some committed religious nationalists, some ultra-Orthodox Jews like those in Modi'in Illit, and some who just find it a convenient and relatively cheap place to live. But on the whole, it is fair to assume that they are more right-wing and nationalist than the Israeli population as a whole. And we find that in their settlements and communities, the fertility rate is higher than anywhere in pre-1967 Israel. Indeed, at 4.75, it is more than 1.5 children higher than that of the surrounding Arab population of the West Bank. The lowest fertility rate in Israel is in Haifa District, centred around a city renowned traditionally for its secularism and Israeli Labor Party politics.[48]

Israeli women who have completed high school but do not have college or university degrees do indeed have more children than those with degrees. But the difference, at less than half a child, is somewhat smaller than we have observed in the US.[49] This is all the more surprising when you consider that 58 per cent of women in Israel aged 25 to 34 have a university degree or similar, compared with just 37 per cent of men.[50] This suggests that the problem of more educated women and less educated men finding partners does not seem to have the depressing effect on fertility here that it has elsewhere.

Another anomaly about Israel that may give us a clue as to what is going on comes from looking at the question of fertility and marriage. On the whole, in the developed world at least, the lower the fertility rate outside marriage, the lower the fertility rate overall. Hence, in Greece, where traditional mores persist and barely 10 per cent of births are outside marriage, the fertility rate is just 1.34 children per woman. In France, by contrast, most births are outside marriage (around 60 per cent) and women have half a child more than their Greek peers.[51] In Israel, although the share of children born outside wedlock is under 7 per cent, well below the Greek rate, fertility is considerably higher, at over three.[52]

EXPLAINING THE ISRAELI ANOMALY: RELIGION

Israel scores highly on all the metrics of modernity (and certainly has achieved one of the world's highest life expectancies), so why has its fertility rate not followed suit and plunged to the level of Germany or Japan?

The first and most obvious explanation is religion. What makes Israel different is that it is a Jewish state and a predominantly Jewish country. As we have seen, the Abrahamic religions all have a pro-natal doctrine, and Islam and Christianity can be seen at work in places like Indonesia and the Philippines, holding back fertility from falling to sub-replacement, or at least delaying this, unlike in countries like China and Thailand.

This, however, is not a fully satisfactory explanation. For a start, there is nothing inherently more pro-natal about Judaism than Islam or Christianity, and countries traditionally associated with those religions, like Iran or Italy, have fertility rates well below Israel's. As far as Judaism is concerned, contraception is generally discouraged among its strictest adherents, but it has nothing like the universal ban that applies, at least in theory, under Catholicism. For Jews, sexual relations within marriage are not just for the purpose of procreation, but are also for the pleasure of the participants. Contraception and even abortion are permitted if the mother's health is endangered – according to some interpretations, this can include her mental health – and, depending on circumstance, a rabbinic dispensation for the use of contraception can be given once a couple have already had a number of children.

The ultra-Orthodox, as we have seen, make an outsized contribution to the total fertility rate, and there is a close correlation between religiosity and fertility, but that does not explain why even secular Israeli Jews have a fertility rate above that of any other OECD country. So religion can only do part of the explanatory heavy lifting. Another explanation people suggest when trying to explain the Israeli fertility anomaly is that perhaps Judaism is pro-natal for cultural or historical reasons. As far as the historical explanation is concerned, the argument would be that it is particularly about 'replacing those lost' following the Holocaust, in which 6 million Jews were murdered and countless historic communities annihilated.

Certainly, this attitude can be encountered. I once met a Chassid (a type of Haredi Jew) who said to me that when people objected to his large family and asked when he was going to stop, he would reply: 'When we reach 6 million.' But anecdote is not data, and if this were really a valid explanation, you would expect high fertility rates to prevail, and to have prevailed, among Jewish communities beyond Israel. It is certainly the case that ultra-Orthodox Jews outside Israel do have a very high birth rate, but among secular Jews outside Israel this isn't the case. In the US, secular Jews have one of the lowest fertility rates of any religious or ethnic group in the country. American Jews who define themselves by ethnicity but not religion, equivalent perhaps to those Israelis self-defining as 'secular', have just one child per woman, half the level of secular Israelis. American Reform Jews have 1.4, well below the US national average.[53]

With the very large family sizes of the Orthodox and the very low fertility of the non-Orthodox and particularly the totally non-religious, it can be said of Jews outside Israel that they are the same as everyone else – only more so.[54] The low fertility rate of US non-Orthodox Jews might be explained by their relatively high educational and income status, not to mention their tendency to live in big cities, all correlates of low fertility. But if Jewish affiliation or a desire to ensure a Jewish future after the calamity of the Holocaust really acted to motivate large family sizes, we would see this overcoming countervailing factors in the US as we do in Israel. But we do not. And therefore it would seem that neither Jewish religion alone nor a reaction against the population-reducing effects of the Jewish historical experience in the middle of the twentieth century are able to explain what is going on in Israel. In brief, Israel is not the world's only high-fertility, highly developed country just because it is Jewish. Something else must be going on.

CONFLICT FERTILITY RATES

Israel's founding community was engaged in a civil war with the Arab inhabitants of Mandate Palestine before its declaration of independence in May 1948, and Israel was at war with its invading neighbours from the first day of its existence.

Israel has had a peace treaty with one of its neighbours, Jordan, for about three decades, and with another, Egypt, for more than four. In recent years it has widened its network of treaties to other Arab countries, from Morocco to the UAE, and it no longer faces a conventional threat from a surrounding army. So it is not as embattled as once it was. But, as we saw so vividly in October 2023, it still has to face frequent terrorist attacks and worries about the missiles pointing at it from Hamas in Gaza and from Hezbollah in Lebanon, and more existentially about the nuclear programme of Iran, which openly calls for its destruction. Is this situation in some way at the root of the high fertility rate in Israel?

The first and most obvious answer is that it seems unlikely. People under threat worry about bringing children into the world. The blood-curdling and often genocidal threats of Israel's enemies may not be very convincing given Israel's strength, at least when those threats emerge from the likes of Hamas in Gaza, but the country does live under the shadow of a very large Hezbollah arsenal of missiles and an existential threat emanating from an Iran with emerging nuclear capability.[55] Were Israel's fertility rate exceptionally *low*, this would no doubt be cited as a reason.

But if we see Israel's quest for survival as in large part demographic, then we can understand why its citizens are prepared to have a child or two more than is the norm for the developed world. As we have seen, Israel's founding politicians were highly focused on the question of the country's demographic balance. At a time when the vast majority of Jews lived outside Israel, with millions in countries where they suffered persecution and discrimination, and thus might be persuaded to move, immigration was the obvious way to grow the country's Jewish population. With Israel's share of world Jewry now approaching 50 per cent, versus 5 per cent at the country's inception, and with most Jews not in Israel now living in security and prosperity, it is not surprising that today the project of ensuring a Jewish majority is more about Genesis (the creation of new life) than it is about Exodus (immigration).[56]

It would seem, then, that a sense of being beleaguered and surrounded, along with a determination to survive, must explain at least in some part the high fertility level of Israeli Jews. As one Haifa-based demographer put it to me:

> It is ideological. Even the Tel Aviv secularists have a much higher fertility rate than their peers in Europe or America. It is pro-natalism born of our experience with the threat of Arab demography somewhere in mind… If we lived between Holland and Belgium, we would have a much lower fertility rate.[57]

Palestinian demography, within Israel as well as the West Bank and Gaza, has followed the broad outlines expected of the demographic transition and the encounter with modernity. Infant mortality rates in the Occupied Territories, for example, were around 100 per 1,000 when Israel took over in 1967; today they are below a fifth of that level.[58] Life expectancy since the advent of the occupation has been extended by the best part of 20 years. None of this should surprise us. What we see regularly on our television screens are clashes and breakouts of violence, the results of which, even with the recent terrible events, have been at so low a level in recent decades that they have no material demographic impact. By contrast, what we do not see are the day-by-day improvements in the provision of hospitals and public health. The result has been the concomitant expansion of the population. But while fertility rates have now come down sharply, to about three for Israeli Arabs/Palestinians and Palestinians living in the West Bank, and a bit higher in Gaza, even this much lower level of fertility is higher than we might expect from their economic circumstances.

Given the very high levels of education and standards of living among the Palestinians in the Occupied Territories, which are higher than those in many of the surrounding countries, it is surprising that their fertility rates are still somewhat above places like Egypt, Jordan, Syria and Lebanon. This too might be attributable to intentional efforts on the part of Palestinians directly engaged in confrontation with Israel to boost their numbers as part of the conflict.[59] Yasser Arafat, long-time leader of the Palestinian national movement, once declared: 'May our holy womb be blessed,' and forecast: 'We, with our birth rate, will again become a majority here.'[60] Of course we can never definitively show the extent to which these kinds of statements can account for individual births, but at the national level, when other theories seem to fall short, it seems likely that this is part of the explanation.

POLICY AND CULTURE

You might expect pro-natal Israel to offer generous benefits to parents, and particularly to mothers, but this is not so. Israeli women who have been with the same employer for 12 months are entitled to 15 weeks of paid leave and 11 of unpaid. This compares poorly to nearly 60 weeks in Bulgaria, and just short of 40 in the UK.[61] Plans for government-paid paternity leave, which would not affect the mother's rights to maternity leave, are still in their early days and cannot therefore account for elevated fertility rates to date.[62] Israel is not especially generous in terms of child benefit payments or tax breaks for parents, and on assistance with childcare costs it ranks well below countries like Portugal, Korea and Italy, which have much lower fertility rates.[63] Child benefits were actually cut in 2013.[64] The only area where the Israeli state rates especially highly is in the provision of IVF, which is free for the first two children for parents up to the age of 45.[65]

If neither religion nor policy can do much to explain the Israeli anomaly, does that mean that we are left to fall back on the conflict alone? That too has its problems. Not every ethnic or religious conflict gives rise to elevated fertility rates, so why should this one? In the end we are forced to turn to that explanatory catch-all: culture. Pro-natal culture is everywhere in Israel, from the adoring looks babies get on public transport to the proffering of unrequested (and not infrequently irritating) advice to young mothers from strangers. One political scientist told me he thought the provision of support from grandparents was an essential part of the reason Israeli people have more children than those in other countries. Seventy-one per cent of Israeli mothers aged 25–39 receive regular help from grandparents, rising to 82 per cent for the native-born.[66] This is among the highest rates of grandparental participation in the world. But the problem with offering culture as an explanation is that it is often slippery and tends to demand the next explanation. If Israeli grandparents really are unusually helpful to their children when they in turn have offspring, why would that be?

Part of the observed culture in Israel is that early marriage and large families have high status. 'Successful people in high tech have made it if they have a lot of children,' suggests one commentator. 'They have four kids and are proud of the fact that they can afford it. Yachts, private planes and fancy cars are not the symbol here… It's the number of kids.'[67]

If a culture is genuinely pro-natal, there is no one strand that can explain it. But it can perhaps best be seen through the lens of those who identify it and oppose it. One woman who suggested that she would prefer to continue to lead a free, single life was warned: 'Your night-life experiences will be over soon, and instead of a smiling face of a child awaiting you, you will have a computer screen… good luck for the future!' Another complained that 'women who willingly forgo motherhood sentence themselves to an empty, dull, tormented life, charged with regret and absent of meaning and substance.' But even without such overt pressures, one woman complained that the sheer existence and proliferation of children creates its own pressure, without any need for comments. 'Everyone around me gave birth. Everyone around me were [sic] young women, breastfeeding and with strollers and babies and diapers… You couldn't let any doubts [about having children] come out of your mouth.'[68]

If any other country tried to cultivate a pro-natal culture like that in Israel, it too would doubtless have its dissidents. But without such a culture, it is hard to envisage how a modern society could achieve a fertility rate at replacement level or above. And, as we have seen, without a fertility rate at replacement level or above, it is hard to envisage how a modern society could endure.

But before moving to suggestions as to how to create a more pro-natal culture, it is first to commonly raised objections to it that we now turn.

PART TWO

OBJECTIONS
AND SOLUTIONS

No UK government has ever suggested, explicitly or implicitly, that the fertility rate should be higher, despite the fact that the UK has had sub-replacement fertility for half a century. Other countries have, though: Russia and Hungary have well-known pro-natalist governments, while the Japanese prime minister has introduced new measures to encourage higher fertility, warning of the direst consequences if things remain as they are.[69]

France, meanwhile, adopted its pro-natalist *Code de la famille* in 1939, and its politicians continue to have no hesitation in calling for larger families. The famously liberal and cosmopolitan Dominique de Villepin, prime minister in the first decade of this century, introduced further measures to encourage professionals to have a third child and 'allow a better conciliation between professional and family life'.[70] This was at a time when France's fertility rate, at 1.9, was one of Europe's highest and far from catastrophically below replacement level. More recent falls in France's fertility rate have evoked an unashamedly pro-natalist government response, with centrist President Macron insisting that 'France will only be stronger if it revives the birth rate' as he introduced plans to extend parental leave.[71]

Even after Nazism might have given it a bad name, pro-natalism has also stretched across time and the political spectrum in post-war Germany, from Marxists in the East to Christian Democrats in the West. The communist government of the German Democratic Republic was quite unapologetic about introducing explicitly pro-natalist policies in 1976, ever aware of labour shortages caused not only by a low birth rate but also by so many people escaping west when they could. A generation later, the same pro-natal theme was taken up by Edmund Stoiber, leader of the decidedly anti-communist Christian Social Union in Bavaria (CSU).[72] Beyond Europe, the leftist government of Cuba is encouraging its women to get pregnant and have children.[73] So now, belatedly and in contradiction to its earlier directives, is the communist government of China.[74] It is therefore not just right-wing or populist politicians who can see the problem and wish to address it.

Indeed, even in the English-speaking world, governments are not averse to adopting explicitly pro-natal rhetoric or policies – as we will see in Chapter 9, baby bonuses were adopted in Australia earlier this century.

But in some parts of the world, including in the UK, the idea that politicians and government ministers should call for more births and implement policies to bring about that result is fiercely controversial. When British MP Miriam Cates spoke in 2023 of a national 'malaise' with regard to having children, and lamented the 'collapsing birth rate', she was met by a wall of condemnation. *The Guardian* newspaper suggested she was dangerous and polarising.[75] Her Wikipedia page accused her of pushing an anti-Semitic theory, although of course she had done nothing of the kind.[76] I was called onto a BBC Radio show to defend her against an opponent who suggested that there was something inherently racist about pro-natalism.

A year earlier, when I suggested in an article in the *Sunday Times* that the government should recognise the problem of persistent low fertility, it provoked a strong response and many objections. There were essentially three strands to these objections. The first was feminist, arguing that to call for more babies was somehow an offence against women. The second was environmentalist, contending that more babies would spell the destruction of the planet, and besides, who could want to bring a child into a burning world? The third concerned ethnic minorities, claiming that to call for more children, even if such a call were entirely without any kind of racial or ethnic bias, was somehow racist. The purpose of the next three chapters is to respond to each of these objections in turn. In the last three chapters we will look at what can be done.

5

HOW ABOUT WOMEN?

I N my July 2022 *Sunday Times* article, I suggested that the UK might consider differential tax rates for parents, as are common in much of the world. (In fact this already exists in the UK through the Child Tax Credit, although its effects are among the least generous in Europe.[1]) If the UK Treasury could not afford to reduce taxes on parents, then perhaps it might increase them on non-parents. This suggestion did not go down well. (Though when did a suggestion for higher taxes ever go down well?) But the sharpest response had a feminist edge. 'A plan to tax women for being childless? Welcome to Gilead,' proclaimed HuffPost, referencing the anti-feminist dystopia portrayed in Margaret Atwood's famous 1985 novel *The Handmaid's Tale*, despite the fact that in the article I had spoken about differentiating tax between parents and non-parents, making no distinction between men and women.[2] The following week, the *Sunday Times* published a riposte to my article under a headline insisting that 'A man can't fix childcare. Only a woman can.' An article in a magazine called *Stylist* was headlined: 'Paul Morland's viral *Sunday Times* piece shows it's easier to blame women than to make meaningful change'. Needless to say, there was nothing in my article that could be construed as 'blaming women'.

It is understandable that the hackles of some feminists rise when pro-natalism is discussed. They associate choice-less childbearing with a dark past in which women had few or no rights. They are conscious of the reactionary resistance to the spread of contraception and the desire on the part of some – although, I would respond, a small and largely irrel-evant few – who would wish to see the rights women have gained over recent decades reversed. Although the world now faces the impending catastrophe of too few births, we should not forget the historical travails of women who could not determine the pattern of their own fertility, nor should we ignore the reality that many women in the world today con-tinue to face this challenge, even if, mercifully, their number is declining. It has recently been estimated that 160 million women worldwide cannot access effective contraception, and it is perfectly valid – indeed laudable – for the international community to continue to work with local governments and people to change this. But this is no longer the reality for most of the world – prior to the outbreak of Covid, an estimated 77 per cent of contraceptive needs globally *were* being met.[3] In Bangladesh, for example, the use of contraception among women of fertile age rose from 8 per cent to 62 per cent between 1975 and 2014.[4] This has gone hand in hand with the extension of rights to women.

The historical background of forced pregnancies and child-bearing, which is also the current though diminishing reality in some countries, has had a formative influence on feminist attitudes. And it is reasonable for feminists to be sensitive to any suggestion that we should return to those sorts of conditions, for example by removing access to contraception, as the communist regime in Romania did in the 1960s. But while we do not want to return to an era of no choice, nor move into an age when freedoms are removed, we do need to go forward to a time when creating life is more frequently chosen. The challenge we face is to adapt ourselves to the changed circumstances of the world, in which most women can access contraception, and most countries have a fertility rate below replacement. And whatever feminism's historical positions on the question of children, there are several good reasons why we should see twenty-first century feminism as being perfectly congruent with a more positive approach to parenthood.

First, and most importantly, there is the simple expedient of listening to what women actually say they want. In the UK and the US women have around three-quarters of a child less than they say they want. Indeed, women not getting what they want when it comes to having children is a global phenomenon. A 2017 study of the US and 18 European countries showed that, in every one of them, women were having fewer children than they wanted. Almost everywhere in this economically developed zone, the average desired number was between two and 2.5, but in all countries the actual number born was lower. In the case of Spain, it was almost a whole child lower.[5] The gap between those saying they wished to be childless in their early twenties and those actually not having children was in most cases between 10 per cent and 20 per cent of the cohort, so that, for example, in Italy, whereas only about 2 per cent of women in their early twenties said they did not want children, more than 20 per cent had not had them as they approached the end of their fertile years.[6] Research from Iran shows that women in every age group are more likely to undershoot than to overshoot their fertility goals.[7]

There is evidence that the desired fertility of younger cohorts is declining in some places – but so too is their actual fertility, so the gap between desire and reality remains and is likely to continue to do so.[8] In other places, including the US, the desired number of children is not falling, while the actual number born per woman is, so the gap is in fact widening.[9] For whatever reason, women's desires in terms of their fertility are not being realised. The following, from a *Guardian* article, is typical: 'I'm a 49-year-old woman. I work hard, own a home and live a fairly good life. My problem is that I can't help but feel regretful that I never had children. I can't quite believe this is how my life turned out. When I was younger I ached for my own child.'[10]

Second, there is also a correlation between patriarchy and small families rather than large ones. In countries like Korea and Japan, where women are given educational opportunities but are then denied the chance to progress in the workplace if they also have a family, they choose not to have a family. Similarly, where traditional attitudes to marriage and child-bearing put a taboo on extramarital childbirth, fertility is generally lower than where attitudes are more relaxed, as we have seen. The path to higher fertility rates in the developed world lies through greater female emancipation, and in particular through enhanced rights and opportunities for women to enjoy a career alongside motherhood.

Third, what is true with regard to social norms and the workplace is true of the home. In developed countries, far from higher fertility being associated with the patriarchal household, it is quite the reverse. Some evidence shows that where men do a greater share of the housework, fertility rates go up. As one review of the literature on the subject put it:

> Recently, studies have documented a connection between gender equality in the domestic sphere and its impact on fertility. This strand of research shows that in families where women do the majority of the housework, the likelihood of progression to higher order births is rather low... On the other hand, in households characterized by a more egalitarian division of housework where husbands increasingly share domestic responsibilities, fertility tends to increase.[11]

This may be the reason why countries where men play a greater role in undertaking household chores, such as those in Scandinavia and northern Europe, experience a higher fertility rate than those where more traditional male roles predominate, such as in Italy and, as we have seen, South Korea. However, other research has questioned the robustness of this link.[12]

Fourth, for feminists to advance women's interests then there need to *be* women. Once abortion becomes widespread and ultrasound scans are the norm, selective abortions take place in societies where male children are valued more highly than females. We have already seen what this means in Korea, where there is a wide disparity between the numbers of men and women in certain age cohorts. But it is not just South Korea: it is estimated that in South Asia, 7,000 fewer girls are born than boys *every day*. Apart from any feminist or wider ethical considerations, this gives rise to practical issues. For every 1,000 men in Punjab, there are only 900 women.[13] Globally, selective abortions may account for a shortfall of as many as 200 million girls.[14] Such practices are now common among South Asian communities in the West as well. As a result of sex-selective abortions, the world is simply less female than it would be if it was left up to nature alone, and the way to reverse this is by having more children.

Taking these disparate factors into account, we can see the contours of a feminism that reacts positively to birth, embraces both choice in principle as well as the choice to have children in practice, and which calls for society to support women in bearing future generations. Of course, such a feminism should put female autonomy and choice front and centre, but it does not assume that choices around childbearing necessarily mean less childbearing. This is a feminism that the world badly needs, and on which the human future depends.

My own small contribution was a response to a question posed to me when I was recently in Seoul. What, I was asked, should Koreans be doing to encourage a rise in their birth rate? 'Should we be doing more to celebrate motherhood?' the journalist asked me. 'No,' I replied, as a father who has done his share of nappy-changing for his children, and is now doing it for his grandchildren. 'We should be doing more to celebrate *parenthood*.'

6

HOW ABOUT THE ENVIRONMENT?

T HERE is within the environmental movement a streak of misanthropy that often expresses itself in the form of anti-natalism. A human concern for the environment – for clean air, fresh water and a benign climate – is a reasonable and indeed laudable sentiment that reflects human self-interest as well as an appreciation for nature as an end in itself. Concern for the well-being of other species represents what philosopher Peter Singer calls an expanding circle: first we are concerned for ourselves and for our families, then for a wider family circle and the immediate community, then for the imagined communities we call nations. Ultimately our altruistic concerns spread to humanity as a whole and then beyond to all creation.[1] This is seen as an ethical progression. It also reflects an understanding that just as no man is an island, neither is a species. We are reliant on other species and jointly reliant on the environment that supports and gives life to us all.

It would be a real conundrum, however, if concern for the environment necessarily required the demise of humanity, or at least a huge fall in human numbers. Short of a disaster such as a pandemic much more severe than Covid, humanity cannot reduce its numbers other than through falling birth rates, and this means the reshaping of the demographic pyramid such that society is put under intense strain through ageing, declining workforces, rising dependency ratios and spiralling government debt. So we might be faced with a choice between two unpalatable fates: a socio-economic crisis on the one hand, and an environmental catastrophe on the other. Ultimately the latter would lead to the former in any case. No society can prosper, however healthy its demography, if its environment is collapsing around it. The objective of this chapter is to show that the conundrum is a false one, and that a thriving environment need not involve human decline.

But before we get to this, we must address a separate argument: that things are now so bad from the point of view of the environment that we have no business bringing new life into the world, since we would be dooming these children to an apocalypse of pain and danger.

THE DISASTER DELUSION

It is not my intention in this book to minimise in any way the challenges humanity has ahead of it. But we need to firmly reject the notion that the world is just too awful for us to contemplate inflicting it on new people by having children. This notion is being widely diffused, is widely believed, and would appear already to be having a negative and increasing impact on fertility rates. But it's not true.

One environmentally concerned American thirty-something, contemplating whether or not to have children, declares: 'I wanted to have a child, but I was also looking at the planet and thinking: "Well, what kind of future will we have if there's more of the same?'" Another US-based prospective mother ponders whether or not to take the plunge into parenthood and expresses her fear: 'It's coming partly from a place of love for my hypothetical child... I want to protect them from suffering. Not that life is ever free from suffering, but... what of the joys and peace and goodness that make me happiest to be alive will be accessible in twenty, thirty, forty years?' A third prospective mother says: 'With the uncertainty of the world right now – it doesn't feel safe.' Reflecting on the parlous state of the environment she has decided, 'I wouldn't want to subject my children to that.'[2] She divorced her husband on account of their differences when it came to the question of having children, and married a man who also wished to remain childless.

A 2021 US-based survey of those not wishing or expecting to have children found that the environmental question was a modest but not immaterial part of their decision: around 6 per cent of those wishing to remain childless cited concerns about the environment or the state of the world more generally.[3] But a more comprehensive survey of people aged 16 to 25 in countries in the developed and developing worlds suggested that, given the prospect of climate change, 39 per cent were hesitant to have children at all. The number was highest in the two developing countries covered in the survey, Brazil and the Philippines. It is perhaps surprising that this percentage was not even higher: the same survey showed that 75 per cent thought that the future was frightening, and 55 per cent thought that humanity was doomed.[4]

But according to this logic, I should never have been born, and nor should anyone of my generation. Two years before my birth humanity teetered on the edge of self-destruction during the Cuban missile crisis. Although the crisis was over by the time of my conception, the danger of nuclear obliteration remained salient for another quarter of a century until the demise of the Soviet Union. This has not entirely gone away for good and probably never will, as nuclear weapons cannot be un-invented. My own existence depended on the decision to have children not only of my parents in the 1960s, but of my grandparents and great-grandparents, and so on. The prospects of my immediate ancestors at birth could be portrayed as being as grim as my own, if not more so. My father was born in 1922 in a defeated, resentful Germany wracked by hyperinflation; my mother arrived 11 years later, when Hitler had come to power and Europe was on the path to war and genocide. As for my grandparents, the youngest was born in 1912 as the clouds of the First World War were gathering, while the oldest turned up in the middle of the late nineteenth-century economic depression that cast a shadow over much of Europe. Despite this ill timing, my parents and grandparents lived or are still living worthwhile and satisfying lives. I am sure that none of them would have wished never to have been born, and are pleased that their parents did not decide that the world at the point of their conception was just too awful to bring a child into. I imagine that most readers would be able to construct a similar narrative about themselves and their forebears.

In fact, based on the current data, there has never been a better time to be born. An awareness of these facts might dispel some of the gloom among those of childbearing age now. When I was born in the UK in the mid-1960s, 21 children in a thousand died before their first birthday, already a fraction of what it had been a few decades earlier. When my first grandchildren were born in the early 2020s, the infant mortality rate was down to a little over three per thousand.[5] So a child born in Britain today has *one-seventh* of the probability of dying in infancy compared to a child born when I was. Globally, over the same period, the rate of infant death has fallen from 120 per thousand to fewer than 30.[6] Similarly, the chance of a woman dying in childbirth has reduced by a full third since the year 2000 alone.[7]

Looking at the other end of life, a UK-born child back in the mid-1960s could expect to live into his or her early seventies. Since then, a whole decade has been added to life expectancy at birth, from the early seventies to the early eighties. The UK was already at that point a relatively rich and developed country, and progress has been faster in countries that were then poor. Globally, life expectancy at birth is around two decades longer than it was when I was born.[8] Even where progress has stalled, life expectancy is, by historical standards, astonishingly long.

If life were nothing more than a painful struggle, any increased chance of living longer would not be a good thing – but again, the data point in precisely the opposite direction. Since the Second World War, per capita daily consumption of food has risen across the globe from an average of just over 2,000 calories a day to just under 3,000.[9] This is despite a tripling of the world's population. As recently as 1950, around two-thirds of the world's people were malnourished.[10] In the first two decades of the twenty-first century, the share of humanity that is underfed fell from 13 per cent to 8 per cent.[11] For much of history, the vast majority of people were probably underfed at least for extended periods. Those of us who have never known real hunger can only start to fathom the mountain of human misery that has been avoided by the extraordinary improvement in our ability to feed ourselves.

It is not just the food supply that is improving. Humans are becoming more peaceful. Deaths in wars have not followed a straight path since 1945, but there has been a clear downward trend.[12] Deaths from natural disasters have fallen progressively since 1900, so although the population of the world since then has quintupled, the number of people dying as a result of such catastrophes has fallen by more than 90 per cent.[13] This means that the chance of an individual dying due to a natural disaster since the era when my grandparents were born is down by around 98 per cent. This may surprise many of the young, doom-laden prospective parents cited above, but it should come as no surprise. Better educated, better housed and generally richer, we are far better able to foresee, anticipate, counteract, avoid and extricate ourselves from hurricanes and floods than we were in the past.

Even on more purely environmental measures, the truth is very far away from humanity's being 'trapped in a giant gas chamber', as a spokesperson from the environmentalist group Just Stop Oil claimed in 2023.[14] Globally, the number of people dying from air pollution was estimated at 6.7 million in 2019.[15] Around half of these deaths were the result of household air pollution, generally involving the burning of kerosene and biomass in antiquated domestic stoves. But the technology to ensure that this is reversed is already available; it just needs to be deployed more widely. When it is, the experience of today's richer countries will be reflected globally. In Manchester in the UK, once a byword for industrial filth, not a single death related to air pollution was recorded in the first two decades of the current century. During those 20 years, only one death due to air pollution was recorded for the UK as a whole.[16] When a UK death is traceable to air pollution, it makes national head-lines, which testifies to its rarity.[17] In the year 2000, almost 40 per cent of the global population did not have access to clean drinking water. Today, a little over two decades later, that figure has fallen to about 25 per cent.[18] Even war-torn and drought-ridden Somalia, one of the poorest countries on earth, has seen infant mortality drop by more than a third and life expectancy extend by more than a decade since the mid-1980s.[19]

Other measures of human well-being and flourishing point sharply upwards. For most of human history, the majority of people had next to no formal education and were illiterate. For most of us in developed countries, where almost everyone can read and write, the debilitating effects of such illiteracy are hard to imagine, including the inability to participate in cultural or political life, or to make even the most modest steps in fulfilling your potential. Since 1820, global illiteracy has fallen from 87 per cent to 12 per cent.[20] There is every reason to believe that this trend will continue until illiteracy comes to be seen as a strange feature of a distant past, as rare in Sierra Leone as it is today in South Korea. At the other end of the educational spectrum, global enrolment in tertiary education has risen from around 10 per cent of school-leavers in 1970 to more than a third today.[21] Literate and more educated lives are invariably materially and culturally richer lives.

My intention here is not to suggest that humanity has attained paradise on earth, nor that we should do anything other than strive to continue to improve human survival, pros-perity, health and education. Rather, it's to show that, unsteady and incomplete though it may be, human progress has been astonishing, especially in the past few decades, and continues to be so. If prospective parents were more aware of facts like those cited above, they would marvel at how much better life has become, and would likely feel far less fearful of the future. It is a paradox that, precisely at the time when things have grown so much better, many people have come to perceive the world as so much worse. Anyone who believes that on account of the current state of the world it is still irresponsible or cruel to bring a new life into it will have to admit that it was far more irresponsible and far crueller for his or her parents to have had children, and so much more for *their* parents in turn, since the prospects for new life today are so much better than they were in the past. If, given the state of the world now, we are ill-advised to have children, our ancestors must have been crazy or wicked to have done so. But in fact, the opposite is the case. We should be grateful that they did, and we should console ourselves with the fact that we will bring our offspring into a far brighter and richer world than our ancestors could have envisaged.

PEOPLE AS POLLUTERS

I hope I have shown that the world is not too awful for a prospective parent to bring a new life into – or, at least, if it is awful, it's much less awful than it used to be, even in the recent past. But is the damage that a new life can do too awful to impose upon the world?

The most immediate concern is man-made global warming. By emitting gases, predominantly from fossil fuels, humans are warming the planet. It has already warmed by about one degree since pre-industrial times, and is projected to go on warming, with disruptive effects on human and other life forms. Besides the general effect of warming, emissions are causing climate change with more disruptive irregularities in the weather, including more intensely hot summers, as well as floods and hurricanes.[22] Is any of this an argument for us to continue reducing our birth rate?

The first thing to say is that, so far, none of this has had a calamitous impact on human existence. As we have seen, there are more humans living better lives than ever before. And even recent warnings have been proved wrong. A 2004 academic paper suggested that crop yields would fall because of climate change – a calamitous prospect, even if such falls were modest, given the ongoing growth in global population.[23] A 2007 paper concluded that 'all quantitative assessments show that climate change will adversely affect food security'.[24] But in fact, in the first two decades of the current century, and despite climate change, food output rose globally by about 50 per cent.[25] This was far faster than population growth, and therefore provided far more food per head, as discussed above. Crop yields, or output per hectare, have grown fast in the past 20 years, meaning that the extra output has not necessarily required further human infringement on those spaces currently left for nature.[26] Today, to produce the same amount of food, less than 30 per cent of the land required in 1960 is needed.[27] While we should continue to worry about the loss of priceless biodiverse tropical rainforest, this progress can give us confidence that the human impingement on nature can be halted and even in some places reversed.

There is also more uncertainty about the effect and speed of climate change than is generally thought, and many predictions of the past have not materialised. In 2012, Cambridge

University experts predicted ice-free summers in the Arctic within four years.[28] They have not yet occurred. The same source now suggests that it will happen by the 2030s.[29] Other sources suggest that the Arctic 'could' become ice-free in the summer by 2050.[30] The view at the time of writing (July 2023) puts the sea ice for the current year at the higher end of the range compared with most recent years.[31] Meanwhile, the stable or expanding sea ice over the Antarctic is apparently the result of the same processes of climate change and global warming.[32] As, it would seem, are the very recent record lows.[33] The government of the Pacific island state of Kiribati was so concerned about loss of land to climate-driven rising sea levels that in 2014 it bought land in Fiji to house its population.[34] But a 2023 study showed that in fact, the islands that constitute Kiribati and thousands of others in the Pacific are growing in area.[35] Although global warming means more people dying of heat in extreme weather events, it also means fewer dying of cold. Since global deaths from cold exceed those from heat almost tenfold, rising temperatures are estimated to have cut the overall number of temperature-related deaths.[36]

My point is not to express scepticism about climate change, but simply to point out that there is still a great deal that we have to learn about this urgent and important subject, and that sometimes what we read in the papers and hear in the broadcast media is more alarmist than the data can justify. The science is clear enough that we should continue with efforts to reduce our carbon emissions. But it does not point indisputably towards the kind of calamity that should make us try to abolish the human race. However you interpret the data on climate change and global warming, it still does not amount to a case for anti-natalism. True, the complete elimination of humanity would end man-made carbon and other greenhouse gas emissions at a stroke – but it would be a strange way to save humanity, by eliminating it.

We must also consider progress that has already been made. The UK's annual per capita emissions are 4.6 metric tons, barely a third of the US's. The UK may have largely outsourced its manufacturing, which has helped reduce its emissions, but Germany, still a major manufacturing power, achieves a per capita level of emissions just above half that of the US. Denmark, a cold country where much domestic heating is required, has a similar level of per capita emissions to the UK's, despite a higher living standard.[37] Even adjusting the data to reflect consumption rather than production, UK emissions per head have still fallen by 40 per cent in the 15 years between 2005 and 2020, and other European countries have made similar gains.[38]

The comparison of regions within countries is almost as telling as comparisons between countries. In London, emissions per capita are significantly less than half the level in Scotland. There are several reasons for this. London's population is entirely urban, and city dwellers live in smaller, often better-insulated homes, and are more likely to use public transport.[39] (To be fair, London's milder climate also requires less use of domestic heating.) So reducing emissions does not necessarily mean a fall in living standards, or a reduction in population. Londoners overall are considerably wealthier than Scots. Danes do not have a much lower GDP per capita than Americans, and some would say have a higher quality of life.

Looking at changes over time, in the UK, per capita income grew by 516 per cent and emissions by 354 per cent between 1850 and 1985. Since 1985, per capita GDP has risen a further

70 per cent or so, while emissions have fallen by around 40 per cent.[40] This has in part to do with a huge rise in the use of renewable energy (wind and solar power), a shift from coal to less polluting and carbon-emitting gas, and improvements in the fuel efficiency of car engines, boilers and home insulation. The latest domestic gas boilers are almost twice as efficient as the worst older models – and that is before considering better insulation or the introduction of heat pumps.[41]

Although the US remains a leading emitter, its record too is impressive. US greenhouse gas emissions peaked 20 years ago, despite strong economic growth since then. On a per capita basis, emissions have fallen by almost a third over the same period.[42] The fuel efficiency of vehicles on US roads rose 69 per cent between 1972 and 2017, and that was before electric vehicles had made any material impression.[43] The most efficient non-electric and non-hybrid vehicles today are three times as fuel efficient as the early 1970s average.[44] China, which is rapidly installing alternative energy capacity, is expected by some to experience a peak in emissions in the next few years and to reduce emissions by 80 per cent by the middle of the century.[45]

We are getting better and smarter at a whole range of activities, which means we can reduce our emissions without reducing our population. New technologies that are far more efficient at producing lower or no emissions have been developed and are now being rolled out, so that within a relatively short period, significant further gains should be achieved. The World Economic Forum reckons that solar power costs fell by 80 per cent between 2010 and 2019.[46] Nuclear energy has great potential for carbon-free energy if its politics and economics can be sorted out. Battery energy storage costs are estimated to have fallen by over 70 per cent between 2014 and

2020.[47] Breakthroughs in hydrogen or cold fusion may – or may not – come to our rescue. Human ingenuity is astounding and we have already seen extraordinary progress in the science and technology that will allow us to continue to lead lives of reasonable material prosperity while preserving the planet and without having to reduce the number of people living on it.

It is also worth remembering that global population growth has already halved, from more than 2 per cent in the late 1960s to less than 1 per cent today. Further falls are inevitable. In advocating an average global fertility rate of two to three, I am not calling for a never-ending population explosion but rather for the sort of steady global population growth that should be reconcilable with continuing falls in greenhouse gas emissions.

THE ULTIMATE RESOURCE

In order to combine gently rising numbers with planetary environmental health, it is clear that we are going to have to rely on technological innovation. But innovation is not something that just happens. The processes, systems and cultures that cultivate technological change are complex and only partly understood. It certainly helps to educate a country's entire population, and to value the input from all its citizens, while the internet is an extraordinary resource for speeding up cooperation between people working on the same scientific or technological problems: the era when those collaborating on research and development projects in different countries required phone calls, faxes and written correspondence sent by snail mail seems very distant indeed, although this only began to change during the 1990s.

Arguing with Malthusian Paul Ehrlich in the 1970s and 1980s, economist Julian Simon was convinced that natural resources would not run out and that we would find new ways around shortages. The classic case was oil. American cars were notorious gas-guzzlers until the early 1970s, when fuel was cheap. Successive oil price shocks (plus more recent concerns about fossil fuel emissions) stimulated investment into making cars more fuel efficient. The same high prices of petrol at various points in the cycle have in turn stimulated exploration efforts that have meant that despite heavy usage, global oil reserves today are about three-quarters higher than they were 30 years ago.[48] It may be that we do not want to – indeed must not – burn all that oil, but the point is that, as Simon put it, human inventiveness is the ultimate resource. As the saying has it, the Stone Age did not end because we ran out of stones. The oil age will not end because we run out of oil. To deploy a historical analogy, in the 1860s leading British economist William Stanley Jevons worried about the country running out of coal.[49] Today, with hundreds of years' worth of coal reserves still under British soil, coal mining has more or less entirely ceased and will probably never recommence.

Just as great technological progress in the past means that now is the best time to bring a child into the world, we should have confidence that humanity can find solutions to the present and the future, including combating climate change, without having to reduce our numbers. One of the main motivators of technological progress is the kind of economic system that allows free markets and rewards risk and enterprise. Profit-seeking companies in the West, not central planners in communist Moscow, saw rising fuel prices in the 1970s as an opportunity to profit by producing more fuel-efficient cars. Fuel costs rose, more fuel-efficient cars were produced, and the public was motivated by economic interest to buy them. That is how market economies work. But what is also required are inventive young minds and risk-taking providers of capital. The concern now is that as our societies age, there is a doubly negative impact on our ability and tendency to innovate. First, there are fewer young people around to think, create and invent. And it is invariably the young who do.[50] Innovation seems to trail off in a society once it has fewer than four people of working age per retiree, a point long passed by most developed countries now.[51] Second, capital that is predominantly at the service of the elderly seeks low-risk assets such as government bonds, rather than the high-risk channels that fund new ideas. Higher-risk investments with higher long-term potential returns but great riskiness make sense for those aiming for the largest pension pot at a distant future point. They can afford possible ups and downs. For those approaching the point where they will have to start living off their retirement capital, or for those already doing so, losses cannot so easily be borne, so a lower-risk approach makes more sense.

We can already see this at work in Japan, which is just about the world's oldest country by population. During the immediate post-war decades, Japan was famous for its inventiveness, often developing the ideas of others and commercialising them. Whether deeply original or mainly adaptational (the latter is in any case often underrated), Japanese inventiveness, along with the country's industriousness and organisation, was at the heart of its rise to a prominent economic position; it was even seen as a rival to US global economic dominance.[52] In the 1990s, the first decade of its demographically driven economic slump, Japan's private sector research and development spend went from almost two-thirds of the US's to barely two-fifths. In the same decade, patent applications from Japan went from double those in the US to barely a third.[53] In the two decades to 2018, the number of Japanese students enrolled in science- and mathematics-related subjects declined by 17 per cent.[54] As the absolute number of Japanese students keeps falling, we can expect this decline to carry on.

It is true that Japan continues to innovate heavily in issues to do with the management of the elderly, hardly surprising given the age of its own population and their pressing needs: from 'care robots', which are supposed to assist in looking after the elderly, to sensors and alarms to cover thinly staffed night shifts in care homes.[55] But even in this field, we can expect the Japanese to lose their edge as their society has fewer and fewer young innovators. And this loss of innovation, along with ageing, will recur in other countries that fail to renew themselves demographically. Which means that a declining population, involving a rapidly declining number of young people, could see the whole global effort to decarbonise fail due to lack of innovation.

We cannot be sure which breakthrough will be game- changing – whether carbon capture, or new forms of fuel, or something we have not even begun to think about yet. But we can be sure that if solutions do emerge, they will arise from the minds and cooperation of young people. These young people might be being born now. Or, given the world's nose- diving fertility rates, they might not. Julian Simon was keen to stress that we should think of people not as consumers of the future, jostling each other in ever-greater numbers for a share of an ever-declining pool of fixed resources, but more as future producers and thinkers, finding new ways to meet human needs and facilitate human flourishing, and grow the collective pie. New people are not just extra mouths. They are extra hands. And extra brains.

MOVING PLACES

Those who refrain from having children for environmental reasons continue to exist as consumers in the economy. They take a train requiring a driver, throw out rubbish requiring a bin collector, attend a hospital requiring a nurse and read a book requiring an author. If they do not fly because they wish to preserve the planet, they might take a train to a nearby holiday destination, and therefore still need the services of people to build the train and run the railway. If they desist from eating meat, they will still eat plant foods, some of which are highly processed, which also require labour for their production and distribution. To use an analogy, they are like someone who deplores agriculture and refuses on principle to farm, but still eats. Someone has to do their farming for them. This is not to decry people changing their consumption patterns for environmental reasons, but rather to point out that regardless of what these changing patterns mean for the non-human resources involved, they still demand the input of human labour.

That being the case, when people in rich countries wish to consume labour but are not prepared to produce it, they invariably turn to immigrants. Goods can be imported, but many services require the on-the-spot presence of those performing them. And because the consumers of labour in rich countries tend to draw in immigration from poorer countries, they are responsible for moving people from low- to high-emission countries, where their individual emissions (along with their overall standard of living) will rise. By the time an average Syrian moving to Germany has achieved the living standard of a typical German, their emissions will have increased sixfold. For a typical Ghanaian immigrating to the UK, the increase is more than seven and a half-fold. For a Guatemalan moving to the US, it is more than 13-fold.[56] Failing to have a child and resolving the resulting labour shortage through immigration is a displacement activity rather than a solution that really reduces emissions. And there are other limitations to immigration as a solution to our demographic woes. These are the subject of the next chapter.

7

HOW ABOUT IMMIGRATION?

O F all the blanket accusations thrown at pro-natalists, none is stranger, or more potentially damaging, than the accusation of racism. 'Conservative calls for women to have more babies hide pernicious motives,' proclaims the headline of a recent *Observer* article. The article goes on to say of British pro-natalists that they 'may be desperate for people to have more babies, but only the right kinds of people... Theirs is a policy programme linked to fears about immigration.'[1]

When I wrote an article advocating more births in the UK, I was explicit that I was not calling for higher birth rates from one group or another in our multiracial and multicultural society. As I have often pointed out, many ethnic minorities in the UK and in other developed countries have fertility rates as low as the population as a whole, or lower. A mixture of low birth rates and intermarriage, for example, has resulted in the UK's Afro-Caribbean population being the only ethnic minority that shrank between the 2011 and 2021 censuses.[2] The fertility rates of UK Sikhs and Hindus are well below replacement level and appear to be similar to that of the white British, while the fertility of UK Muslims, although higher, is also falling.[3]

Cases of discriminatory pro-natalism have of course existed and continue to exist. While the Chinese government is now encouraging its Han population to have more children, it is reportedly forcing IUD implants on women of the Uyghur minority and other minority groups.[4] Social security payments for children in Lebanon are not paid to those of Palestinian origin, even if they and their families have been in the country for generations.[5] In the later years of the Soviet Union, enhanced child benefits, supposedly to be paid across the country as a whole, were rolled out first in the ethnically Russian areas and never reached minorities in places such as Uzbekistan.[6] Romania under Ceaușescu, it is claimed, winked at abortions and the availability of contraception in ethnically Hungarian areas while imposing draconian pro-natalism on the ethnically Romanian.[7]

But just because some communist regimes or governments in the Middle East are, or have been, racially or ethnically discriminatory in their encouragement of childbirth, this should not condemn pro-natalism itself as inherently discriminatory. Some pension systems have been accused of being discriminatory against women; this is hardly an argument against the provision of pensions per se.[8] The fact that buses in some parts of the US were once racially segregated is hardly an argument for shutting down all bus services.

Indeed, pro-natalists celebrate and hold up as examples those African women who choose to bear two or three children on average even when they have the means to follow their European, East Asian and North American sisters in having fewer.

The accusation of racism directed at pro-natalists can perhaps be dated to an era when low fertility rates were mainly a concern of white people. People of European extraction were the first to enter the demographic transition (when mortality rates plunged and the population expanded) and the first to exit it (with fertility rates falling and the population stabilising in size). There was a time when some white racists worried that the birth rates for whites were falling while those of every other racial group were still high. This was similar to those who fretted that the upper classes started to adopt birth control, when contraception had not yet filtered down to the less well-off.[9]

But as we have seen, those days are long over. The Japanese were the pioneers of very low fertility rates, the consequences of which they are increasingly experiencing. Today the South Koreans are the world champions of reluctance to bear children. And low fertility has spread to places where it would once have been least expected, and which are decidedly not 'white': in St Lucia, for example, fertility rates are now at Japanese levels of about 1.3 children per woman. Hispanic women in Puerto Rico have fewer than half the children born in overwhelmingly white South Dakota, while the fertility rate in West Bengal is lower than the fertility rate in France.[10]

Perhaps pro-natalism has been tarred with the brush of racism because it has been promoted by right-wing regimes and is generally associated with the political right. But left-wing dictators from Stalin to Mao to Castro have also been dedicated to boosting the birth rate. Today and in recent years governments of the right, like those in Hungary and Poland, have been promoters of larger families, but so also (after an about-face) is the government of the People's Republic of China. So are many members of the EU, and not just those with governments which can be categorised as right-wing populists, but also countries with more mainstream governments, from Finland to Spain.[11]

In Western countries like Britain, pro-natalists are sometimes accused of racism, perhaps because those of us advocating more births often suggest that the solution to our labour shortages cannot be found by resort to endless inflows of immigrants. Our argument, however, is nothing to do with race, and is instead based on the dynamics of demography.

THE LIMITS OF IMMIGRATION
AS A SOLUTION

A society's supply of labour depends on the number of people of working age. Its demand for labour depends on the number of people in total. The relation between the two is the old-age dependency ratio: the number of people of retirement age vs those of working age.

As fewer children from past decades come through adolescence and into the workforce at the same time as the number of retirees continues to grow, the overall workforce shrinks while the requirements of the economy for labour does not. After the Second World War in Britain, for example, the demand for labour was intense. Not only was reconstruction desperately needed after the devastation caused by bombing, but the population was heavily reduced by wartime losses. The armed forces continued to use much of the potential workforce through National Service – conscription of young men aged 17 to 21, for up to two years, was not fully wound down until 1963.[12] The workforce was also reduced by the fact that during the interwar period, the fertility rate had fallen to historic lows, reaching around two children per woman by 1939. The post-war baby boom fixed the problem with a large inflow into the workforce in the 1970s and 1980s, which contributed to the historically high unemployment rate in those decades. But as the baby-boomers have started to retire and the low fertility of recent decades has meant the net inflow into the workforce has shrunk to a tenth of what it was 30 years ago, the result is a labour shortage.[13] This is a phenomenon we see repeated across much of the developed world, including the US.[14]

One way to ameliorate this would be to delay the age of retirement, but that can only offer a limited, one-off shot in the arm for the labour force, and tends to meet great resistance. Another is to import workers, which Britain began to do in the late 1940s, and is doing now in great numbers. But immigrants, too, grow old and retire. The original *Windrush* generation, for example – those of working age who arrived in the UK from the West Indies in the immediate post-war years – have long retired and now require just as much health and social care as others of their age. The fertility rate in the islands they left was high, at five or more children per woman by as late as the 1960s, but the fertility rates of West Indians in the UK, as we have seen, have adapted to local levels (and indeed are now even lower back home). So we have failed to achieve any lasting solution to the problem of persistently below-replacement fertility rates. This does not mean that we should not be appreciative of those who have moved to developed countries to work, enriching their host societies in so doing. But using this method to prevent dependency ratios from falling will require ever more immigration as the elderly cohort grows. In contrast, a fertility rate at or slightly above replacement rate ensures a healthy population pyramid, with enough young workers to replace retirees.

RELATIVE WEALTH AS AN ATTRACTION TO IMMIGRANTS

Britain's fertility rate was low in the interwar period but recovered after the war during the baby boom that ran until the 1960s. The fertility rate went sub-replacement in the early 1970s, which meant Britain increasingly felt the pinch in the labour markets during the 1990s. Despite continuing deindustrialisation and the export of manufacturing jobs to China, unemployment, the great economic plague of the previous decades, steadily fell. The recession in the early 1990s never resulted in the level of unemployment seen in the early 1980s slump, nor did it last for as long. Similarly, the rise in unemployment during the financial crisis at the end of the first decade of the twenty-first century was lower than in previous recessions, and then declined to new lows.[15] (Clearly this is positive in that it avoids unemployment, a waste of human potential and a source of misery. But although politicians still talk endlessly about the need for jobs, our new reality is increasingly going to be one in which the need is for workers.) It was also from the late 1990s that immigration began to take off and reach record-breaking levels.[16] Much of the immigration came from the countries of the former Eastern bloc, liberated from communism from the late 1990s. Their people were relatively well educated, free to leave their homes and, thanks to the UK's early adoption of EU freedom-of-movement regulations, able to work in the UK from 2004.[17]

The recent past has lured the UK into a false sense of security. The fall of the Berlin Wall and the sudden availability of a large, well-educated and poor workforce that was willing and able to move to the UK was not 'normal', nor can we expect this combination of factors to be repeated. The UK has long been home to a population of Polish origin, in significant numbers since at least the Second World War, providing the family links that can make it so much easier for a new wave of immigrants to enter and settle down successfully. The UK was a country familiar, at least to some extent, to Poles, and even if they did not already speak English, it was a language well worth learning. But, most important of all, the UK was a country where earnings would be much higher than at home.

But Poland has prospered since it was freed from the constraints of state socialism and could start to benefit from access to EU markets. In 2000, Polish wage levels were around one-seventh of those in the UK. By 2019, they had grown to between a quarter and a third.[18] Adjusted for prices, Poland's per capita GDP has risen since 2002 from a little over one-third to nearly four-fifths of the UK's.[19] Working in the UK remains relatively more remunerative for Poles, but the gap has narrowed and is likely to continue to do so. To be motivated to leave your family and move to a new country requires some incentive. If you are leaving a place that is politically stable and more or less respects your human rights, the motivation is likely to be economic. If that economic pull diminishes, fewer will come. There are still almost 700,000 Poles living in the UK, even after Brexit.[20] But we should not expect that number to continue to rise even if admission rules meant it could.

We have already seen how the developed world has lost some of its lead over the developing world in measures of well-being, such as low infant mortality rates and long life expectancy. Indeed, there has been a general economic catching-up by poorer countries. While the wealthiest countries continue to draw in people from poorer nations, the pull will diminish if the gap between countries' economic well-being continues to narrow. As an example, for many decades the British mainland was a major attraction for immigrants from Ireland, drawn by higher wages. But wages are now higher in the Republic of Ireland than in the UK, so the economic pull has diminished. In recent years, emigration from the UK to Ireland has consistently outstripped migration in the other direction across the Irish Sea.[21] Newly arrived Irish immigrants were a mainstay of the British workforce from the middle of the nineteenth century until the end of the twentieth. They are no more.

A similar phenomenon can be seen at work in other European countries. Between the wars, there was large-scale immigration from Spain and Italy into France. In the early 1930s there were nearly 400,000 Spaniards and nearly a million Italians living there.[22] But more recently the countries of southern Europe have caught up and the draw has become less strong. In the immediate post-war era, many Portuguese left their homeland to seek higher wages in northern European countries like Luxembourg, and today they represent almost 15 per cent of the population of the Grand Duchy.[23] But with major rises in living standards in Portugal, the incentives to leave are now far lower. For the wealthy countries of northwestern Europe, their great lead over the countries of the south and east in economic terms has been significantly eroded. They would have been unwise to think that they could call on immigrants from poorer countries like Italy, Spain, Portugal and other poorer parts of Europe forever. And they would be similarly unwise to think that they will be able to rely forever on a higher standard of living than that of countries outside Europe. Adjusted to reflect prices and the cost of living, the share of the world economy commanded by current EU members has roughly halved since 1980, from 30 per cent to not much more than 15 per cent.[24] As economies beyond Europe rise and prospects improve, their populations will prefer to stay at home. But it is not just a question of converging economics. It is also a question of converging demography.

WANING BIRTH RATES BACK HOME

We have seen how immigrant communities' birth rates tend to converge with those of their host societies. 'Why would I want to have kids and be tied down to a man forever? Watching my mom work two or three jobs to provide for my brother and me also made me realize that having kids is a huge financial burden,' says one first-generation immigrant in California who came from Mexico as a child. A Brazilian living in Canada says: 'From an early age, I've always liked my quiet time, and I love traveling. I like my hobbies… It didn't make sense to have kids, because we have a very long wish list of where to go.'[25] These women are typical of people who move from high- to low-fertility countries and adopt the low fertility rates of the latter. Frequently, fertility rates have fallen back home too, so that today in much of the West Indies they are considerably lower than in the UK. Previously high-fertility lands that used to send out emigrants have simply started having far fewer children.

In the case of Poland, a country of nearly 38 million, its potential emigrants were large enough in number to make a difference to a country like the UK when they became free to leave and free to enter from 2004. At that point, there were almost 6.5 million twenty-something Poles, those in the age group most likely to want to start a new life in a foreign country. By 2020, this number had already declined to fewer than 4.5 million. By the end of the century, it will have halved from the current level. Already over the past 15 years or so, the old-age dependency ratio in Poland has risen from just over 20 per cent to just over 30 per cent. By 2050, it will be just over 60 per cent, according to the UN's best estimates.[26] Not only are the economic incentives for Poles to come to the UK diminishing, there are fewer of them at the age most likely to come. What's more, the need for them at home is rising. Poland has had a fertility rate below 1.5 since the late 1990s, so it is going to have severe labour shortages of its own.

The same sort of demography is at work in Romania. The number of people in their twenties is already down by a third from 2007, when Romanians were first allowed to travel freely to the UK and other countries in the EU prepared to open their gates earlier than strictly required by Brussels. The number of Romanian twenty-somethings will decline a further 25 per cent towards the middle of the current century. Again, the root cause is fertility rates, on a bumpy decline since people found ways around Ceaușescu's coercive pro-natalism in the 1960s, resulting in a below-replacement rate for decades. The Ukraine war may well mean another generation of east Europeans heading west, but once the war is over, many are likely to return home. If they don't, it would be disastrous for Ukraine, which will need them to rebuild the country.

Just as the narrowing of the economic gap applied first to poorer Europeans and then to the wider world, so does the closing of the demographic gap. In the early 1970s, women in India had around four children more than women in the UK, a total fertility rate of about six as opposed to around two. Today, the gap is around a third of a child, and although the fertility rate of the UK is continuing to fall, India's is falling faster. Similar data can be shown for France as against Algeria, or Turkey as against Germany. The same is true of Mexico and the US. In the early 1970s, Mexican women were having four children more than women north of the Rio Grande. Today, the child premium in Mexico is less than one-third. More Mexicans have been going back to Mexico than coming the other way for a number of years.[27] Today, the main inflow of Latinos into the US is from poorer countries in Central America with higher fertility rates. They too are now seeing falling fertility rates: El Salvador's is similar to the US's, and Guatemala's, although higher, has halved since the mid-1990s. In time, their economies will also narrow the gap with the richer north.

It is vain too to think that Africa will forever wish or be in a position to offer up its young. 'If Kenya is typical of the path that Africa is on,' as one pair of commentators puts it, 'then expecting African parents to produce the babies that people in other parts of the world aren't having is unrealistic.'[28]

THE SIZE OF THE DEFICIT

Since the early 1970s, much of the developed world has seen fertility rates below replacement level. This has meant more modest flows of people into the labour force, which have been supplemented in many cases by immigration inflows. But as we look to the future, the level of immigration required is going to be much greater than in the past because of the length of time that low fertility has continued and the depths to which it has plunged, as well as because of the shape of past population booms. The biggest cohort of the UK baby boom, those born in 1964, will only start retiring en masse in the coming years as they hit 60. Their removal from the workplace over the next decade will be the sharpest and most profound loss of workers we have experienced. Slightly earlier cohorts who are already retiring were quite large, and the pain is already being felt. Normally, with years of sluggish economic growth and mass immigration behind us, you would expect there to be mass unemployment. Instead, we face tight labour markets. Further falls in fertility rates now will make the situation even worse in the future.

In South Korea, sub-replacement fertility hit a decade and a half later than in the UK. But despite this, it has since fallen much lower, with South Korean women now having close to half the fertility level of UK women. That is why, to retain its dependency ratio, South Korea would require unprecedented levels of immigration. Its working-age population at the end of the current century is forecast to be around 13 million. To retain today's ratio, it would need to boost that by an additional 34 million without increasing the number of retirees.[29] Plenty of other countries have followed or are following the steep downward path of Korean fertility, which means that the demand for immigrants from low-fertility countries will rise relentlessly – precisely as the potential supply shrinks, since fewer countries are producing large numbers of children per woman.

This points to another potential problem of using immigration as a solution. Polish workers coming to the UK from 2004 were relatively well educated and skilled. They could fit productively into an advanced economy. But the remaining countries with high fertility rates and the potential to provide immigrants to the developed world are increasingly low-income, and generally their people have low levels of education. The highest levels of fertility in the world today are in Niger, at just about seven children per woman. Per capita income in Niger, which is broadly representative of economic productivity, is less than one hundredth of the level in the US.[30] Transplant a worker from Niger to the US, provide him or her with the level of capital deployed by a US citizen, and give him or her the same level of education (if his or her arrival is not too late for such education to be effective) and the worker's productivity will soar. But it will be a lengthy and expensive process, not the easy transition of workers from relatively well-educated, middle-income societies to which many developed countries have grown accustomed.

CULTURE AND REACTION

The history of race relations in the former colonial powers and in the US is a major topic largely beyond the scope of this book. But it is clear that mass immigration from the developing world has resulted in a backlash at certain times and in certain places. The UK vote for Brexit in 2016 can be understood in part as a reaction against immigration.[31] The same is true of the Trump presidential victory in the US later that year, when the Republican candidate's promise to build a wall along the Mexican border was his most iconic pledge.

Across Continental Europe, from Sweden to Italy, parties of the far right have taken power or come close to it based partly or largely on promises of lower immigration. France's Marine Le Pen gained twice the share of the vote in the 2022 election run-off than her father received two decades earlier, testimony to a rising tide of right-wing populism in the heart of a continent with fast-changing ethnic demography.[32] Governments in Poland and Hungary have long resisted EU pressure to take more migrants, and they have won popular backing and elections as a result.[33] In the most recent election in the Netherlands, the largest party, headed by Geert Wilders, ran on an anti-immigration platform. In democracies, we cannot ignore popular sentiments that translate into votes and political outcomes.

But this is far from being an issue only in the countries that have traditionally received immigrants from the developing world. 'Should we not be making every effort to preserve our ethnic and cultural homogeneity?' a Korean journalist from a major Seoul-based publication asked me in a 2023 interview when I suggested that immigration might be at least part of the answer for South Korea's demographic woes. A survey suggested that on a scale of one to five, where a score of five represents strong agreement, the average South Korean scores 3.77 in agreement to the statement: 'I am proud of having long maintained a racially homogenous nation.'[34] In 2023, only around 3 per cent of the inhabitants of Korea were not ethnically Korean.[35] Although East Asian countries are not a natural destination for immigrants from South Asia and Africa, it is not only cultural and linguistic difficulties that prevent them from coming, but also a degree of resistance within the host countries themselves.

Similarly, in February 2023, Tunisian President Kais Saied complained about the arrival in his country of 'hordes of irregular migrants from Sub-Saharan Africa', who had come to Tunisia, with all the 'violence, crime, and unacceptable practices that entails'. This was, he went on to say an 'unnatural' situation and part of a criminal plan designed to 'change the demographic make-up' of his country and turn it into 'just another African country that doesn't belong to the Arab and Islamic nations any more'.[36] Despite widespread international condemnation, the president expressed similar sentiments again a few months later.[37]

Such sentiments are not uncommon across the African continent. Tens of thousands of Asians were expelled from Uganda in 1972.[38] Two million West African migrants to Nigeria were summarily expelled in 1983, half of them Ghanaians. 'If they don't leave, they should be arrested and tried and sent back to their homes. Illegal immigrants, under normal circumstances, should not be given any notice whatsoever,' insisted the country's president.[39] Hundreds of Zimbabweans fled South African xenophobic riots in 2015. However much liberals may insist on cosmopolitanism and deplore the refusal of societies to absorb immigrants, such sentiments are far from universal, either at home or abroad. To assume immigration can be the complete answer to shortages of people of working age, forever and without limit, is politically naive and unrealistic.

BIOLOGICAL IMPERIALISM

Even if an endless supply of highly productive potential immigrants *were* available to every country that is already, or soon will be, short of workers, however, we should question the morality of relying wholly on such an inflow.

Today we rightly deplore the arrogance of nineteenth-century Europeans in carving up Africa between them, yet we are currently engaged in an exercise that history might consider equally arrogant in its assumptions, as well as highly damaging in its effects. The people of the wealthier countries of Europe, along with Canada, the US and Australia, assume that a shortage of labour deriving from their own low birth rate can be made up to meet demand by bringing in people from poorer countries. Indeed, they have become dependent upon such people, and are set to become even more dependent on them as the impact of ever-lower fertility works its way through the labour markets.

It's true that immigrants, whether from Nicaragua or Nevada, or from Mali or Marseilles, are coming of their own free will. Indeed, many are risking their lives to make the journey and to improve their economic lot. But while individuals themselves may be enormously enriched by the opportunity to move from the developing to the developed world, and their families and local economies often benefit from the remittances they send home, their emigration also represents a loss of human capital to the countries they have left. Those who make it out tend to be the young and the most energetic and enterprising. Often, they are the best qualified. We are depriving the countries they leave behind of their talents and skills.

In the UK, for example, a shortage of doctors and other healthcare workers has resulted in an overseas recruitment drive. The UK is not supposed to poach doctors from developing countries where the need for them is great.[40] Yet according to one calculation, there are more Ghanaian healthcare workers working in the UK than in Ghana.[41] In Ghana, despite progress in recent decades, life expectancy is still more than 15 years shorter than in the UK, and infant mortality nearly ten times as high. The UK has over ten times more doctors per capita than Ghana. Moving trained physicians from Ghana to the UK represents therefore a very regressive and inequitable distribution of human talent. And this is but one example of what happens when people in the rich world, for whatever reason, do not produce the labour force of the future but continue to require a vast array of services involving labour.

IMMIGRATION IS NOT THE ANSWER

Attracting immigrants to reverse the effect of population ageing may have been a solution for wealthy, relatively small populations in the past. But it is not a solution for a society like China even in the short term. China's size means it would require vast numbers of immigrants, while its relative poverty, even today, ensures it is unlikely to be able to attract them. And while people from the declining number of high-fertility countries in sub-Saharan Africa often speak English or French and see living in Europe as a desirable goal, they are much less likely to speak Chinese or to view China as an attractive or feasible place to which to emigrate. There are not remotely enough potential migrants on the planet to keep China's dependency ratio steady if its people choose to have a fertility rate not much above half the level required to replace themselves.

Even as a temporary palliative, then, immigration can only work for certain countries in certain circumstances. First, receiving countries have to be rich enough to be able to attract large numbers of immigrants. Second, there have to be enough places where fertility rates continue to be high, thus creating potential sources of migration. If the post-war West Indian immigration to the UK happened now, for instance, it would cause population collapse there. Third, the natural decline in dependency ratios resulting from sub-replacement fertility rates must not be too steep or the rate of immigration required will be too rapid to ensure integration and social harmony and to prevent the kind of populist backlash we are seeing in much of Continental Europe. Fourth, the receiving countries have to have cultures that attract immigrants from high-fertility countries, and into which they are likely to be accepted; Japan, despite its population woes, still has very limited migration.

In recent decades, a relatively small number of countries, where these criteria have been met, have been in a position to solve their labour shortages through immigration.

But even where immigration does assist in countering the effects of long-standing low fertility, declining birth rates and rising dependency ratios, there are several reasons why we in the developed world should not be as reliant on immigration as we have become. The ease with which we have been able to attract highly skilled workers to our shores has in some part been the result of unusual historical circumstances that will not be repeated. We may be able to continue recruiting poorer people from the developing world for decades to come, but we will be increasingly drawing them in from countries with low labour productivity. If immigration continues on its current scale, we will have to devote resources to the education and training of migrants, while claiming a shortage of resources for young couples having children at home. We will also need to house them, while home-born citizens who do not have children attribute their choices to a lack of housing. Meanwhile the rapid ethnic change arising from immigration is feeding a rising wave of right-wing populism which might take draconian action against further immigration. And – perhaps most importantly – we should question the morality of effectively relying on other countries to do our childbearing, child-rearing and education for us, creating a labour force that we then take over, depriving them of the human capital they have invested in and urgently need themselves.

We have seen that low fertility rates are spreading across the globe. Once exclusive to the wealthiest and most developed countries, we now see them even in quite poor ones. Humanity as a whole is about to record below-replacement fertility rates. Moving people around may suit the needs of one group of people, the world's wealthiest and most privileged. But as a plunging birth rate goes global, it can hardly be a solution for humanity as a whole. Nor is it fair.

8

WHAT TECHNOLOGY
CAN DO FOR US

I N 1811, workers in the wool and cotton industries began
a wave of machine-smashing in the English county of
Nottinghamshire that soon spread northwards to Yorkshire.
These industries, we now know, were the launch pads of
the industrial revolution, the application of steam power to
machinery and transport that was eventually to transform
the lives of people across the globe – and is still doing so.
At the time no such panoramic view of history was available, certainly not to the workers who were being drawn into
Britain's expanding textile industry. What they could see, and
what they were reacting against, was the introduction of new
technologies. These, they feared, would deprive them of their
livelihoods and render their skills obsolete. A few years later,
the trouble started up again. Behind this movement of industrial sabotage lurked a mythical figure, holding out like Robin
Hood in Sherwood Forest five or six hundred years earlier, by
the name of Ned Ludd. The machine-smashers were severely
suppressed by the government, and in 1813 wide-scale pros-
ecutions led to a number of hangings and deportations. Ever
since, those opposed to the introduction of new technology

for fear of losing their means of earning a living have been known as Luddites.[1]

People have invariably tended to resist new techniques and technologies. It's a conservatism that has grown out of a resistance to change, based on a calculation of the risk involved in any kind of novelty in a traditional society. Where a rash decision or miscalculation could result in the loss of the margin between harsh existence and utter penury, or even between life and death, such conservatism made sense. But since the industrial revolution, changes to the means of production have occurred with extraordinary speed by historical standards, and people have grown accustomed to them. As Karl Marx and Friedrich Engels put it in the 1840s, in one of their best-known descriptions:

> Constant revolutionising of production, uninterrupted disturbance of all social conditions, everlasting uncertainty and agitation distinguish the bourgeois epoch from all earlier ones. All fixed, fast-frozen relations, with their train of ancient and venerable prejudices and opinions, are swept away, all new-formed ones become antiquated before they can ossify. All that is solid melts into air, all that is holy is profaned, and man is at last compelled to face with sober senses his real conditions of life, and his relations with his kind.[2]

Luddites past and present can be derided, but it was far from clear to the textile workers of the early nineteenth century that the technologies that threatened their earning power would eventually lead to incomes and a standard of living for their descendants that they could hardly have imagined. And even if they had known this, it may well have made no difference at all to their opposition to the introduction of technological novelty. By some reckonings, working-class living standards did not start to rise meaningfully in England until the 1880s. Going without dinner today, and being forced to leave your home tomorrow in the interests of a pay rise for your great-grandchildren more than half a century later, would hardly have seemed like a good deal to those threatened by deskilling and unemployment in the 1810s.

Nevertheless, with the luxury of hindsight it is now clear to us that Luddites were wrong-headed, at least insofar as they thought that mechanisation would take away the opportunity to work. We can now see that ever since the dawn of the industrial revolution, new innovations tend to call forth new demands for work and workers. That hardly seemed obvious back in the days of Ned Ludd. If machines could do the work of men and women, and much faster, who would need to employ men and women? But in fact, a vast requirement for factory hands and other related workers was created, and although life in the factory was dangerous and unpleasant, the productive forces unleashed meant clothing became vastly cheaper for ordinary people. And there were advantages to an urban life and regular income, however grim and grimy early cities may have been and despite the precarious nature of industrial employment.

Similar processes have been at work ever since. The motor car overwhelmingly reduced the need for the vast industry involved in the use of horses for transport: horse breeding, buying and selling; growing and trading fodder; manufacturing and selling saddles and bridles; making and fitting horseshoes, and so on. In 1900, London was home to 300,000 horses. Today, it has fewer than 200.[3] Yet the stables where they were looked after are not rotting and empty: many have been converted into luxury mews homes. The fields that once grew their fodder now produce something else, or have been used for housing or schools. For the most part, the individuals involved in equine trades are long dead, but in a busy and dynamic economy, in all likelihood they would have found alternative employment as horse-related jobs disappeared. The horse economy is now a niche industry. That is the nature of the modern capitalist society that Marx and Engels were describing, and which today fits their description even better than it did when they wrote it.

The implications of all this for the pro-natalist case are significant. As a society ages, with fewer people coming through to join the labour force while the demands of the older population continue to grow, we are going to run out of people to do the work required. Indeed, we have already reached this stage in many countries, as we have seen.

But what if advances in technology mean that, very soon, we will not require people to do the work, because, one way or another, machines will be doing it instead? Luddites were protesting against technology replacing labour, seeing this in a wholly negative light. But what if such a development could be our saving grace and come to the rescue of humanity now that humanity seems to have lost interest in reproducing itself? People would still have fewer children than they want, and they would miss out on the life-enhancing experience of parenthood. It would not answer the calls of those religious and philosophical outlooks that see the creation of new life as inherently good. But at least it would mean that we do not run out of people to do the jobs that need doing. Instead of our offspring undertaking all the practical tasks that the economy requires, machines would perform these instead. I believe that this kind of techno-optimism (if optimism it is) is misguided.

HERE WE GO AGAIN

The Luddites, as we have seen, may have been right to think that the nascent industrial revolution was not in their personal interest, but they were wrong to believe that it would mean an end to the demand for labour. Today there are more than 30 million people at work in the UK, almost three times the entire population at the time of the Luddite revolt.[4] Since then, people have nevertheless been predicting the end of labour, or at least a very considerable reduction in the demand for it. The great economist John Maynard Keynes famously forecast in his 1930 essay 'The Economic Possibilities of our Grandchildren' that with the continuation of productivity gains, people would be able to work very short hours in a couple of generations.[5] The number of hours worked in most advanced economies certainly has fallen in the near-century since Keynes's essay was penned, but not by nearly as much as he might have expected. In the US, hours worked were almost exactly the same in 2017 as in 1938. In Germany, by contrast, they dropped by nearly 40 per cent over the same period. Most advanced countries fell somewhere between the two. But nowhere did they fall to the extent that Keynes thought possible.[6]

Nearly 20 years after Keynes's forecasts, American mathematician Norbert Wiener was warning: 'If we can do anything in a clear and intelligible way, we can do it by machine.' Machines would advance to the point that, at least with regard to the factory labourer, 'he is not worth employing at any price'.[7] Contrary to Wiener's expectation, this was the dawn of a golden era of high employment and good wages for industrial jobs in the US.

Attitudes have varied towards the potential replacement of human labour by machinery, and a lack of things for us to do in the economy. Some, like the Luddites, fear penury. Others, like Keynes, look forward to a time when people can pursue the arts and educate and cultivate themselves, freed from the daily grind of needing to earn a living. Should such a time come to pass, it is not clear how people would cope and whether it would be good or bad for humanity. Much would depend on the financial arrangements, and how the product of the economy was distributed. (If all the returns went to the technology-owners, most people would be unable to buy the output of the economy, creating what Marxists would call a crisis of overproduction, and Keynesians a lack of effective demand. A minimum guaranteed income might then be required.) Much, too, would depend on human psychology and whether we could preserve our self-esteem and mental health in a world without work. The psychological damage that we know unemployment inflicts does not augur well.[8] But perhaps it would be different if everyone were in the same boat, and if the lack of work lost its stigma and did not have relative material poverty as a consequence.

In any case, the promise of ubiquitous leisure seems always to be before us, but it has never quite materialised. It is true that agriculture requires dramatically fewer people than it once did. In France, nearly 60 per cent of the workforce was engaged in agriculture in 1800, while today the share is less than 3 per cent.[9] Yet France produces more food and her people are better fed than ever, and France continues to be a net food exporter.[10] Machines and technology, from the tractor to pesticides, have allowed an enormous increase in the output of food while requiring less and less labour. The same has happened in manufacturing, where mechanisation has greatly reduced the need for labour. Germany continues to be one of the world's leading manufacturing export countries, responsible for more than 5 per cent of the world's manufactured goods, while home to only 1 per cent of its people. Yet the share of workers in manufacturing in Germany has more than halved since 1970.[11]

But despite the waning labour requirements of industry and agriculture, people continue to be needed. And the new jobs, multifarious though they are, tend to be more appealing than the jobs they replace. I once met a Jakarta taxi driver who told me how much pleasanter it was to drive a cab, even in the traffic chaos of the Indonesian capital, than to squat for hours in a Javan paddy field in the blazing heat as his father and grandfather had done. And he was proud that his son was working in an air-conditioned office.[12] A similar story could be told the world over. Agriculture was traditionally back-breaking, leaving those engaged in it prematurely aged. The same can be said of coal-mining and much industrial work. The death toll in factories was high. Today's work, even if not always enjoyable or pleasant, is far more likely to take place in a clean and pleasant environment and carry far less risk of injury or death.

The labour shake-out in agriculture and industry has not resulted in mass unemployment, as was once feared. This is thanks to the extraordinary rise in the demand for services, greater than would have been expected even 40 or 50 years ago. Some of these apparently new services do not in themselves involve new technology, but have been facilitated by it. For example, Uber and similar apps have grown the number of people using taxis, and therefore the number of people supplying taxi services: there were over 90,000 more taxi and private vehicle drivers for hire in 2022 in the UK than in 2005.[13] Airbnb may have somewhat reduced the demand for hotels, but overall it has stimulated the accommodation market, with more people taking trips and staying away from home, and more individuals earning money through providing hosting services. And of course, the technology required to support these apps consumes a great deal of labour, albeit more of the brainy and less of the brawny kind: between 2017 and 2023, the number of people working in tech in the US increased by close to 19 per cent, or around 1.5 million.[14] Many of the jobs they have been doing did not exist in anything like their current form until quite recently. When I started in the workforce in the 1980s, and indeed for years after, I had never heard of an email. When I became a parent in the 1990s, I had never heard of an app. The creation and maintenance of this new technology has involved, and continues to involve, millions of hours of work. The accountancy firm PwC calculates that 30 per cent of today's jobs will be at risk by the mid-2030. But new jobs by the millions are just as likely to be created.[15]

The workforce changes so quickly that often parents, and certainly grandparents, do not understand what it is that the younger generation does. Some of this may be the relabelling of tasks that may not actually have changed that much (think of 'personnel' being replaced by 'human resources'), but much of this is the result of increasing specialisation, similar to what the economist Adam Smith noticed happening in a pin factory, or of the spawning of entirely new fields. My wife has worked as a consultant specialising in governance and pay, areas that have become increasingly important since compensation for senior executives has come under more scrutiny from shareholders and particularly regulators. A friend of mine has a son who is a project manager at the Center for Effective Altruism. The title of both the job and the institution would have baffled my grandparents. One of my sons-in-law describes himself on his LinkedIn page as a 'QA Automation Engineer, providing automated test coverage to our data infrastructure'. I needed him to explain to me what this means and I am still not sure I understand. So my sense is that the tendency of human societies and economies to invent new and ever more complex and sophisticated ways of requiring labour is not about to end.

It might be suggested that the supply of labour creates its own demand, and if that supply of labour evaporates for demographic or other reasons, so will the demand, without anyone being much worse off. There are lots of jobs that we could manage without if the price of labour rose too high. But we should hesitate before deciding that the new jobs appearing now are somehow frivolous or unnecessary just because they were only created yesterday, or because we do not always understand what they involve. The Luddites would not have understood the jobs involved with railways, something future generations came to depend on. Today most of us get very frustrated if the Wi-Fi goes down at home, but a few decades ago we had never even heard of the internet. And just because our great-grandparents may have lived in places without regular rubbish collections, or their great-grandparents in places without a proper sewage infrastructure, this will not stop us feeling that civilisation is collapsing when these services cease because there is no one to carry them out.

'EVERYWHERE BUT IN THE PRODUCTIVITY STATISTICS'

If we were on the verge of an era in which technology was going to replace labour wholesale, we would expect one of two things to be happening. Either we would see the current workforce, more or less static in number, producing an economy of vastly more value. Or we would see a similar-sized economy vastly reducing the need for labour. Some combination of the two would probably be more likely, with a rapidly growing economy requiring fewer hours of work and fewer workers. One way or another, we would see output per hour worked, or labour productivity, growing exponentially. If we were on the verge of a techno-breakthrough in which labour would be replaced almost entirely, we would see labour productivity rising sharply.

But in fact, in developed countries using cutting-edge technologies, we have seen almost the very opposite. Labour productivity, which once rose year-on-year, has been decidedly sluggish. The UK has been a particularly poor case. Productivity grew 3.7 per cent a year in the three decades after the Second World War. It grew 2.4 per cent annually in the three decades from 1977 to 2007, but in the following 15 years, productivity grew at less than one tenth of that pace.[16] Productivity is higher in other developed countries, such as Germany, but even there the growth rate has been on a long downward trajectory.[17] US labour productivity rose by about a third in the first decade of the current century and by barely a tenth in the second.[18] The measurement of labour productivity is itself far from perfect, and the explanations for this stalling are varied and complex. Nevertheless, despite astonishing technological advances in recent decades, the amount of value from an hour of work in the advanced world has increased at a very modest pace. Back in the 1980s, the US Nobel Prize-winning economist Robert Solow said famously: 'You can see the computer age every-where but in the productivity statistics.'[19] It remains the case.

In the 1980s, it was the advent of the age of the personal computer that was supposed to raise productivity, and to some extent in the 1990s it did, although without reducing the need for workers. More recently much has been promised about the rise of robotics. Almost ten years ago, American futurologist Martin Ford wrote a widely acclaimed book called *The Rise of the Robots: Technology and the Threat of Mass Unemployment*.[20] Ford pointed out that mass unemployment driven by tech-nological advances had long been predicted and long been wrong. But with the operation of Moore's law – the doubling of computing power every 18 to 24 months – this time really could be different.[21] Advancing technology would not only replace jobs overall, but increasingly it could allow them to be outsourced to lower-cost production centres, meaning that its job-eating impact would likely be felt especially acutely in the rich world. Some 50 per cent of jobs would be susceptible to extinction by machine.[22]

However, as we have seen, the mass unemployment in the developed world that Ford worried about has not material-ised – quite the contrary. Labour markets in the US and other advanced countries are at historically tight levels. This is not to say that a major slump couldn't create unemployment, but even though economies are fairly sluggish, there is little sign of it. The movements of the markets are indeed mysterious, but the substitution of labour does not seem to be more rapid now than in the past. What has changed is demography, and its impact has been to tighten rather than loosen labour markets from China to the Czech Republic.

The robots, then, have not taken over and made us redundant, at least not yet. Part of the reason for this is that even in jobs considered fairly menial, machines are not yet able to perform all the tasks that humans do. Ford talked of robots assisting in care for the elderly in Japan, noting that there was still not much they could do, but looking forward to technological advances from that country.[23] But even in Japan, as a recent MIT report on the use of technology in Japanese care homes put it:

> In short, the machines failed to save labor. The care robots themselves required care: they had to be moved around, maintained, cleaned, booted up, operated, repeatedly explained to residents, constantly monitored during use, and stored away afterwards. Indeed, a growing body of evidence... [found] robots tend to end up creating *more* work for caregivers.

The report found that no robots had been installed in around 90 per cent of homes in Japan.[24] This certainly fits my own observations during my frequent recent visits to an elderly relative in a care home in the UK. I see very little if any activity by the staff that is aided by technology that did not exist decades ago. Monitoring equipment has perhaps improved, allowing less close supervision and so perhaps a slightly lower staff-to-patient ratio. But more likely, rather than replacing staff, this equipment allows existing staff to provide an enhanced service.

Similarly, a few years ago some workmen replaced the roof on my house. They turned up by van, something they may not have done a century ago, but certainly would have 50 years ago. They used my domestic electricity supply, available for the past hundred years. Perhaps the manufacture of the tiles is more automated and less labour-intensive today than in the past. But it would be hard to argue that the whole procedure used far fewer man hours than would have been the case in, say, 1970. We are a very long way from robots collecting our bins, never mind tiling the roof. As fewer and fewer people work in agriculture and industry, the impact of technological labour-saving in those sectors will be smaller on the demand for labour as a whole. It is not obvious in vast swathes of the economy that technology is about to come to the rescue and save us from a lack of people.

Without a doubt some routine tasks will be completed by automata, but even here the results have been so far disappointing. A decade ago, Martin Ford talked about the Google autonomous fleet having driven hundreds of thousands of accident-free miles, although he was aware of the problems ahead – legal as well as technical – before such vehicles could become commonplace.[25] If this happened, millions of professional drivers would be put out of business worldwide and their labour would be available elsewhere in the economy. But this has not yet happened. It was estimated that, by 2021, USD 100 billion of private equity had gone into the self-driving vehicle industry.[26] Some are sceptical that it will ever take off on a mass scale; it may be that driving becomes partly automated but there will always need to be someone at the wheel.[27] In September 2023, *The Economist* proclaimed that 'the robotaxi revolution is upon us'. But it went on to say that the roll-out of the service was uncertain, and in any case, for every robotaxi 'there may be at least one highly paid Silicon Valley engineer tinkering with the technology'.[28] As for self-driving trucks, if they are ever to become a reality a vast amount of work will be required to create them.[29] And even if the professional driver of cab or truck ceases to be required, there is no reason to think that this will be associated with mass unemployment, any more than the replacement of horses with cars was.

In summary, then, no doubt it will continue to be possible to reduce the demand for labour in some areas thanks to developing technology, but it is far from certain that technology will extinguish the requirement for people faster than it creates new needs, any more in the future than in the past.

THIS TIME IS DIFFERENT (AGAIN): THE CASE OF ARTIFICIAL INTELLIGENCE

As I was finishing my undergraduate degree in the mid-1980s, a particularly clever friend of mine was considering taking a master's degree in artificial intelligence. At the time I had little or no idea what this was. Fortunately for him, he did not pursue the idea, but devoted himself to a successful career in pharmaceuticals and finance instead. I say fortunately for him because the field made no breakthroughs for many decades, and however clever he was (and still is), it seems unlikely that his participation alone would have made that much difference.

But now, quite suddenly, breakthroughs have been made. Martin Ford is promising us that artificial intelligence will, in the subtitle of his latest work, 'transform everything'.[30] (Note that, in the title at least, he is no longer promising us mass unemployment.) Many have been excited by the latest releases of ChatGPT, and I used it myself recently. It gave a reasonably coherent and extraordinarily rapid response to my question on why there is such a limited symphonic tradition in French music, and it wrote a good limerick on the subject of love. But when I was egotistical enough to ask it about myself, I was told that I worked for an institution that I have barely heard of and where I have certainly never been employed. Based on an understanding of physics, maths and computer science, as well as psychology, there are those who question whether the dynamic and extremely complex workings of the brain can ever be turned into algorithms that would allow artificial intelligence to replace humans.[31] And even if it could, it wouldn't be able to empty my bins.

Elon Musk – who we have already noted is deeply worried about the decline of fertility and the prospect of population reduction – has also suggested that artificial intelligence will replace the need for human labour, but it is noteworthy that he has not put a date on this.[32] We can, however, put a date on collapsing population size if we make some fairly simple assumptions about fertility and life expectancy.

Of course, the possibility of artificial intelligence replacing labour is now considerable. But the same limitations apply as they do to robots. First, AI may not fully live up to the hype. Second, unless and until we see a remarkable jump in labour productivity, we should be sceptical as to whether it is really replacing labour. And third, we need to check whether, under the reign of AI, labour is more rapidly replaced than new demands for it are created, just as it was in the days of Ned Ludd. At the very least we can surely claim that the evidence is simply not yet available to demonstrate that the practical reason for having children – namely, creating the labour force of the future – has evaporated in the white heat of the latest technological revolution.

9

WHAT GOVERNMENT
CAN DO FOR US

W E live in times when it is automatically assumed that if
there is a problem, there must be something that government can or should do to fix it, usually involving spending
a great deal of money. I was recently in a TV debate with a
young woman in which she asked, 'What incentive am I being
given to have a child?'

Just before the First World War, the British government
received in tax and spent about a tenth of national income.[1] At
the start of the twenty-first century, that share had quadrupled
to around 40 per cent. It has continued to rise since. In this
pattern, the UK is typical of developed countries.[2] And, as we
have seen, with the population ageing, there are few prospects
of this doing anything other than rising further. Neither today's
demography nor the prevailing ideological outlook suggests
that any reduction in the role of government is imminent.

So far, though, there has been no universal call from low-
fertility countries for government action to combat low fertility rates. This is because there is no consensus in many of
the low-fertility countries that they are facing a population
problem. The UK has no demographic strategy and, so far, no

sitting government minister has pronounced that the falling birth rate is a problem. The EU commissioner with relevant responsibilities has explicitly ruled out any kind of pro-natal activism in policy or rhetoric, saying, 'I must first underline that having children is a matter of individual choice in which the EU does not interfere. Indeed this is a personal choice that no government should interfere in.'[3] In the US, you would have to go back to President Theodore Roosevelt in the first decade of the twentieth century to find an explicit statement of governmental encouragement of large families.[4] There, just as family sizes were about to start shrinking in the late 1960s, President Nixon was still being haunted by Malthusian worries about overpopulation.[5] In the last 50 years US administrations have been essentially silent on the subject.

If and when a consensus does emerge that we are having too few children, however, we can expect the obvious next step to be a call for governments to act. Indeed, in some places there is already a long-standing tradition of governments promoting fertility, and government activity in the demographic realm is becoming more common. If we acknowledge that the lack of births is an ever-widening and -deepening crisis for humanity, then we have to consider what role government might play in addressing it, how it might do so, and whether, to date, the record provides any encouragement that this is a problem that the state can fix.

PRO-NATAL POLICY

In recent times, government activism in the field of pro-natalism has been championed by France. This is a continuation of a long history. During the era of French dominance of Europe, from the time of Louis XIV to that of Napoleon (roughly 1643 to 1815), part of France's advantage over its neighbours was demographic. But during the course of the nineteenth century, France lost out to Russia, to the eventually unified Germany and to the UK.[6] So it was not surprising that the French took the matter of population seriously, particularly after their defeat by Prussia in 1870–1, when France's decline was widely put down to demographic factors. By 1916 the 'Groupe parlementaire pour la protection de la natalité et de la famille' (Parliamentary Group for the Protection of the Birth Rate and the Family) was the largest faction within the National Assembly, drawing members from across the political spectrum, and there were big pressure groups outside parliament too. Further falls in the French birth rate, and losses during the First World War, increased French worries about demographic weakness and led to a raft of legislation in the 1930s, particularly the 1938–9 *Code de la famille*, which included welfare payments and tax breaks for large families and a tightening of legislation against abortion.[7]

While pro-natalism was well established in France and acceptable within the democratic framework of the Third Republic, it was the interwar dictators who took it up with enthusiasm and started to give it a bad name. Hitler, Mussolini and Stalin all had an enthusiasm for babies, albeit only babies of the right sort.[8] They introduced packages of incentives and encouragements, medals and accolades, as well as outlawing abortion (an about-turn in the Soviet case after post-1917 liberalisation). The post-war dictators, more likely communist than fascist, tended to be similarly minded. 'Mao loves

179

children,' proclaimed a series of posters in the 1950s and early 1960s. (Only after Mao's death was the one-child policy established in China.) Men responsible for millions of deaths proclaimed their love of births, hoping perhaps that a new generation would meet racial, class or ideological criteria, while a large share of the older generations, who did not, were swept away.

But we should not lose sight of the fact that pro-natalism was not unknown in the post-war democracies either, and was often a policy of the political left. France continued to be in the vanguard, with welfare payment reforms in the mid-1980s under the socialist government of François Mitterrand, for example, aiming specifically to stimulate fertility.[9] In the UK it was the Labour government of Clement Attlee in 1946 that first introduced family allowances, the forerunner of child benefits, albeit with more welfarist than pro-natalist intentions.[10] Today, while the EU itself does not aim to increase fertility rates, some of its members, such as Latvia, do. Its national development plan for 2014–20 insisted that 'increasing the birth rate is important for ensuring the existence of the Latvian nation'.[11]

CONTEMPORARY PRO-NATALIST POLICIES: A GLOBAL OVERVIEW

A UN study in 2019 found that 55 countries had policies aimed at increasing fertility rates, representing 28 per cent of the organisation's membership. This was more than three times the proportion of UN members pursuing such policies in the mid-1970s, and included countries with impeccable liberal and democratic reputations like Portugal, Luxembourg and Finland, as well as the communist dictatorship of Cuba. There are still more countries trying to get their fertility rates down than ones trying to get them up, but whereas in the 1970s there were three times as many such countries, today there are only a quarter more.[12] As fertility falls in country after country and as population decline looms for more and more of us, it is unsurprising that government policy is catching up and increasingly switching from trying to limit population growth to attempting to stimulate it.

Many different approaches have been taken by governments to encouraging fertility. To get a sense of the wide range of these, we will take a look at three cases: Hungary, Australia and China. These are three very different countries, on different continents and with different political systems.

HUNGARY: 'THEY TALK OF ALMOST NOTHING ELSE'

The current Hungarian government is unapologetically pro-natalist. Its leader, prime minister Viktor Orbán, describes himself as an 'illiberal democrat'.[13] The government explicitly links its desire to boost the birth rate with a reluctance to admit immigrants and to retain the current ethnic composition of the country. 'I am the only politician in the EU who stands for an openly anti-immigration policy,' Orbán insisted in 2022. 'This is not a race issue for us, this is a cultural issue.'[14] This puts Hungary beyond the pale for many liberals in western Europe and elsewhere, and for some it gives pro-natalism a bad name. Yet whatever our personal political views of the Orbán administration, for anyone with a concern about the world's demographic crisis, it is well worth examining Hungary as a case study of what has been tried and whether it works.

The current government certainly appears popular: it consistently wins elections. And its policies on family and migration seem to be part of its appeal: 'They talk about almost nothing else here (apart from immigration),' a journalist was told by a friend in Budapest when enquiring about the government's demographic policies.[15] On arrival at Budapest airport, visitors pass by billboards welcoming them to 'family-friendly Hungary'.

The current Hungarian government is right-wing and populist, very different from the communists who ruled between the end of the Second World War and the end of the 1980s. But in terms of pro-natalism, it is following in the steps of its communist predecessors.[16] As early as the 1950s the government clamped down on abortions and the availability of contraceptives, only to be forced to retreat in the face of public objections.[17] In 1967, it introduced the right for women to stay home with their children until the age of three and keep their jobs open, with modest remuneration.[18] Nevertheless, the fertility rate in Hungary fell to below two children per woman in the late 1960s. It recovered somewhat in the 1970s, a bounce-back attributed to the maternity and family allowances introduced by the communists at the time, but it returned to below replacement level in the 1980s and has stayed there ever since. In the 1990s the Hungarian total fertility rate plunged to barely above one, making it among the very lowest in the world. Hungary's population has been falling, albeit gently, for about 40 years, and is now about 10 per cent below its early-1980s peak. Hungary is ethnically fairly homogeneous, with the 2011 census showing the Roma as the largest minority at a little over 3 per cent of the population, though with a consistently higher fertility rate than the majority.[19] A more recent survey puts their share at 7 per cent.[20] The vast majority of the rest are ethnic Magyars.

The current government came to power in 2011. Its minister of families at the time, Katalin Novák, stated clearly: 'Without strong families, there are no strong nations.'[21] (It is noteworthy that Ms Novák, after a decade in family-related ministries, was elected president of Hungary by the National Assembly in 2022.) The new government rapidly introduced generous tax breaks for parents.[22] These were extended in 2018 and mothers of four or more children are now exempt from income tax for life. Children from large families get preferential access to nurseries. Free IVF is being introduced and, in 2020, the government nationalised the fertility clinics, promising to end waiting times for treatment. Since 2015 the government has offered loans of more than EUR 30,000 for couples with, or planning to have, three or more children, to help them purchase a home.[23] (The loans are partly forgiven on the first and second children, and written off entirely once there are three children.) These loans were increased in 2023.[24] One mother, a teaching assistant married to a policeman, welcomes the assistance: 'The loan is brilliant. If it wasn't for this help then we would have to live with one of our parents, or in terrible conditions.' But the terms do create stress: 'We are trying hard for another baby now,' says a mother, currently of one, 'but as the term approaches it does increase the pressure.'[25] Overall, the Hungarian government is estimated to spend around 5 per cent of GDP on pro-natal policies.[26] This is more than three times what it spends on defence.[27]

The government has said it wants the fertility rate to rise to 2.1 by 2030.[28] Although the fertility rate has recovered from around 1.25 to around 1.5 over the past decade, this is well short of the target. There is some evidence that the increase is at best only partly attributable to policy: whereas much of the aid has gone on the birth of third children, these do not actually represent a very large share of additional births.[29]

The data for 2022 suggest that the population continues to decline and that the fertility rate is falling slightly.[30] But traditional social attitudes do seem to be catching on in Hungary. The marriage rate is the highest in Europe and there has been a modest but steady increase in the share of children born in wedlock, contrary to the trend across most of the Continent.[31] So far, however, neither this fact nor the government's rhetoric and spend seem to be having the material effect hoped for.[32] At best, there is some evidence that where new policies are brought in, they create a temporary but not permanent rise in fertility rates.[33]

It is clearly disappointing if a government spends a vast share of the country's GDP on raising the birth rate with such modest results, even where the population seems generally to be behind it. The gap between the aspiration for replacement fertility rates and what has actually been achieved remains about half a child, and Hungarian women only have half the number of children that women in Israel produce. On the other hand, how low would the fertility rate be in the absence of such policies? South Korea has shown us that just when we think a fertility rate can go no lower, we find out that indeed it can. Hungarian women are still having almost twice as many children as women in South Korea, and are far from being the world's lowest child-bearers, as was the case 20 years ago.

But for all its efforts, Hungary has not achieved anything very different in terms of fertility rates to its neighbours Slovakia and Romania.

AUSTRALIA: 'ONE FOR MUM, ONE FOR DAD AND ONE FOR THE COUNTRY'

Moving out of Africa more than 60,000 years ago, humans are believed to have first reached Australia around 50,000 years ago.[34] The European discovery of Australia occurred in the early seventeenth century. By the time Europeans turned up in significant numbers a couple of hundred years later, there are estimated to have been between 300,000 and 1 million Aboriginals living in a space significantly larger than non-Russian Europe.[35] The population then increased with immigrants, first from the British Isles and then increasingly from other parts of Europe and, from the mid-1970s (once the 'White Australia' policy was repealed), from Asia.

Australia has been and remains a highly attractive magnet for immigrants, not only from the developing countries of Asia but also from other parts of the developed world. In addition, in the post-war era, Australia experienced a baby boom typical of the countries of the Anglosphere, with its total fertility rate peaking at over 3.5 children per woman in the early 1960s. Again in line with culturally similar countries, however, fertility rates have fallen, and they have remained below two since the mid-1970s. Thanks to immigration, the population of the country has nevertheless almost doubled in the last 50 years.

From 1912, the Australian government paid out the equivalent of two weeks' wages for an unskilled worker on the birth of a baby; subsequently other welfare benefits to families were granted. In the 1980s, Australia introduced income-related benefits, which were extended in the 1990s, and in the following decade tax allowances were introduced for child-related costs. Statutory parental paid leave was introduced in 2009, which has been extended since, and various other family-friendly policies have been put in place in recent years, underpinning high levels of female participation in the workforce and the widespread availability of part-time work for mothers of young children.[36] As with similar benefits in other parts of the world, these were not necessarily linked to a desire to encourage childbearing, but rather reflected a growing political sense that the state had some responsibility for the welfare of society and particularly for children, and also a desire to facilitate the path of women into the workforce, desirable given high levels of female education, and in order to grow the economy.

But despite a rising population thanks to a high level of immigration, and despite general support for families, Australians have become concerned by their own low birth rate. A 2002 Intergenerational Report published by the government, released when the fertility rate had fallen below 1.75, noted the low birth rate as a potential cause of labour shortages and an ageing society.[37] In 2004, Treasurer Peter Costello, announcing a baby bonus of AUD 3,000 per birth, made an off-the-cuff but long-remembered plea to his countrymen and countrywomen to have 'one for Mum, one for Dad and one for the country'.[38] Years later, pleased that he had at least got the discussion going when he had been in a position of power, he added: 'As a society, we've got to understand this point: we're living longer and having fewer children. This means there just aren't going to be enough people to look after us all in the hospitals and in the aged care centres.'[39]

The bonus was payable to mothers regardless of income, and was raised eventually to AUD 5,000 – although various restrictions were added over time. In particular, with other calls on government spending, it was considered by some to be a poor use of public funds to give relatively large amounts of money to the well-off. A subsequent treasurer justified the introduction of means-testing by insisting: 'We will be targeting our assistance to those people who are on modest incomes.'[40] But the measure was abolished altogether in 2013.[41]

While it is never possible to link behaviour to particular policies with any precision, the Australian fertility rate did rise from 1.75 children in 2002 to just under two children four years later. Since then, though, it has steadily fallen.

A careful statistical study suggests that the policy did have a 'small though positive and significant effect' on fertility rates, and that this was not a temporary or 'compression' effect (that is, it did not just bring forward births that would have happened later anyway, thereby reducing future fertility rates).[42] This is despite the fact that the amounts involved were quite small compared to the overall cost of bringing up a child. Whatever the social science suggests, there is a link in the popular imagination between Costello's policy and the subsequent rise in fertility. As one newspaper article celebrated in 2017, before the current record lows in Australian fertility were reached:

Costello would be happy to know as the baby bonus generation grows up, there will be a record number of Australians coming of age in the next decade. According to Deloitte

Access Economics, by 2030 there will be 360,000 Australians turning 18 years old a year – a staggering 20 per cent increase from the current level of 300,000.

But the article went on, sensibly, to point out that the link is probably less straightforward than most people think.[43]

Responding to the current depressed levels of the Australian fertility rate, there have been calls to reinstate the baby bonus, but they have been ruled out by the current Labor government. 'We've found a better way, I believe, to service the same objective, which is by extending paid parental leave, making early childhood education cheaper so that parents, particularly mums, can work more and earn more if they want to,' Treasurer Jim Chalmers told the National Press Club in August 2023.[44] With its buoyant economy and high standard of living, its relatively small population and proximity to some of the most densely populated parts of the world, migration is likely to be the luxury solution Australia can confidently lean on in lieu of anything effective on the fertility front. But as elsewhere, this has its limitations, and it turns out that the fertility rate of immigrants is even lower than that of native-born Australians.[45]

CHINA: AN INEFFECTIVE ABOUT-TURN

The Chinese one-child policy, which prevailed from around 1980 until its gradual relaxation over the past decade, has been much discussed.[46] My own view is that it was immoral, unnecessary – given the fall in Chinese fertility rates already underway before the policy's implementation and which continued among Chinese populations not subject to the policy after its introduction – and self-harming, as we now see from China's demographic travails.

The first and most obvious effort by the Chinese authorities to reverse the policy was when it was slightly relaxed in 2013, allowing a second child if one of the parents was an only child. There was a more comprehensive relaxation in 2015 permitting two children, which has since been further adjusted to allow three. The whole intrusive apparatus, resulting *in extremis* in coercive abortion, has ceased to operate. As would be expected from a limited amount of short-term pent-up demand for having children, there was a modest uptick in the immediate period after the first rule change, from 1.67 to 1.81 children per woman, according to World Bank data.[47] But by 2019, before the outbreak of the Covid pandemic, the fertility rate was down to a record low of 1.28. China has many of the characteristics that seem to correlate with very low fertility and are common across East Asia: having rapidly urbanised and industrialised; lacking a widespread Abrahamic tradition, notwithstanding relatively small Christian and Muslim minorities; and combining high levels of female education on the one hand with continuing patriarchal attitudes in society on the other.

China's working-age population has already started to decline, as indeed has its population as a whole – by 2 million in the most recent year – and, as we have seen, it is now believed to have been overtaken by India as the world's most populous country.[48] While labour force reductions will be modest over the coming decades, these will create a drag on an economy that grew most vigorously when large numbers of young people were transferring from field to factory. With little by way of a social security net, and with many people having no children to rely on, China may experience depressed consumption as workers save for their old age, which will also have serious economic implications.

In an effort to reverse these effects, the Chinese government has instituted measures that go beyond the mere lifting of the one-child policy. IVF has been made more available, though still only to married couples. Cash payments and tax deductions are offered to those with children, and longer maternity leave is permitted. The government has pledged to improve pre- and post-natal services and has expressed an intention to clamp down on abortions it judges to be medically unnecessary.[49] In China, there are fewer than 10 million births each year and about 13 million abortions, so this is a lever that could be pulled if the government were prepared to do so.[50] There are plenty of precedents for communists banning abortion, starting with the Soviet Union in 1936.

In a noteworthy move, the government is also trying to discourage private tuition, which, as in South Korea, can become something of an expensive arms race, encouraging competitive parents to have fewer children and concentrate more resources on them in order to help them get ahead.[51] But exhortation too, has been found to have its place. In Hubei, for example, troupes of local women are paid to walk around banging pots and drums and yelling pro-natal slogans such as 'Giving birth is an important part of life!' and 'The three-child policy is good!'.[52]

Given the recent nature of the latest policies, it is too early to judge their effectiveness, particularly in view of the distorting impact of Covid on data for the years 2020 to 2023. (If there is an upward fertility bounce in later data, some of this may be due to a post-Covid catching-up.) So it will be a while before a true picture can form. But the data we do have, showing record low fertility rates in China, are not encouraging. A more powerful effect is likely to be the emergence of a culture of indifference or even hostility to the idea of having children, which is taking place across much of the world and particularly in East Asia. 'Getting married and having little chives [*sic*] can only harm my personal development and lower my quality of life,' wrote one Chinese commentator on a local version of Twitter.[53]

SO CAN GOVERNMENT FIX IT?

Case studies of individual countries can only take us so far in answering the question of what governments can do, because just as the causes of low fertility vary from country to country, so too are the solutions likely to differ from place to place.

It is never easy to measure the impact of policies. First, they are changed too often and too quickly. Second, it is impossible to distinguish the impact of policies from the effects of other changes, such as shifting social attitudes and the economic cycle. Third, we cannot be sure about the counterfactual: the fertility rate in Hungary may be disappointing given the huge effort that has gone into raising it, but we cannot say for sure how low it would be in the absence of such policies. Fourth, the chosen metric might have a distorting effect; for example, the introduction of a policy may stimulate births that would have happened anyway but a little later, and so show up in the total fertility rate but not in the total number of births for a given cohort. Fifth, some policies aimed at addressing other issues have an effect on fertility rates: in the UK, for example, the introduction of the family allowance (later called child benefit) in 1945 was aimed at alleviating childhood poverty, but it nevertheless preceded, and may even have helped encourage, a baby boom.

With these provisos, however, there is strong evidence that the provision of childcare is a particularly effective way to boost the fertility rate. A study of different areas in Norway found that completed fertility for a cohort varied considerably depending on childcare availability. Where it was non-existent, the fertility rate was 1.51, but where cover was over 60 per cent, the total fertility rate rose to 2.18. The more childcare there was, the higher the fertility rate. This was for the cohort of women born in the late 1950s and early 1960s, a group who would have received good educational opportunities and who would in many cases have been looking to build careers along-side families. Generous childcare provision in Quebec, along with other family-friendly policies, seems to have helped boost the province's fertility rate in the early years of this century, and it remains a little above the Canadian national average after having been well below it before the policy's introduction.[54] On the other hand, nursery provision has been less effective in Japan, although it may have helped to stave off the country's total fertility rate reaching South Korean levels.

It looks like childcare provision works best where it is combined with a culture that gives women full rights in the workplace, and where men undertake a greater share of work around the home. The evidence on the effectiveness of gen-erous and flexible parental leave, by contrast, is more mixed. Cash transfers seem to have an effect, although this may be short-term and therefore bring forward births that would have happened in any case.[55]

Although this continues to be an area of complexity and confusion, and is likely to remain so, a number of lessons can be drawn. First, without a very particular set of cultural norms such as we find in Israel, it is unlikely that fertility rates will come anywhere close to replacement level unless government is at least prepared to acknowledge the problem of low fertility and to try to do something about it. Second, the possible policies are numerous and varied, and a degree of experimentation is required to find out what works. Continuous experimentation is essential, because even when we find something effective, it will probably not remain effective forever, since society changes. Third, there is a role for perception as well as reality: baby bonuses that cover only a small part of the cost of a child's care can still have an impact. Fourth, if we want women to have children in a world of increasing educational and workplace equality, we must focus on making it feasible for them to combine parenthood and a career: more than anything, this seems to depend on the availability of high-quality, affordable childcare.

In the past, the wealthier a country and the better-educated its women, the lower its fertility. That correlation, though, is unravelling among the wealthiest and best-educated in the developed world, and gives grounds for hope. A survey in Germany cited in Chapter 3 shows that more educated men and women want more, not fewer, children than their less educated compatriots, while US data also cited above show that although fertility falls with increased education as far as master's degree, there is a slight uptick when you get to the PhDs. The world will get wealthier and its women will become better educated. Governments need to work with those trends and ensure that they mean higher, not lower fertility rates.[56]

This can best be done by ensuring that career and family are compatible.

The effort Hungary has made to help young families with housing may also be an important part of a pro-natal package. Living in London, I am very conscious of how expensive housing is. A combination of migration-fuelled population growth, planning restrictions and a significant rise in the wealth of the already well-off (usually middle-aged and older people) resulting from quantitative easing, have made housing unaffordable for many in their twenties and thirties who wish to have children, and there is much to be said in favour of intergenerational redistribution. But we should not delude ourselves that this alone will solve the problem of a low birth rate, especially in highly unequal societies. In parts of the UK where much of the housing is quite cheap, such as large areas of Scotland, fertility rates are particularly low. The same is true of Germany, for example, where housing is affordable in most cities (and childcare is cheap), but young adults are still not choosing to start families.

It goes without saying that, in any democracy, coercion will be ruled out. And stricter controls on abortion are not an effective way to raise the fertility rate: even in Romania in the 1960s and 1970s, the fertility gains following bans on contraception and abortion were only temporary.

If the arguments in this book are correct, and if the collapse in fertility rates is threatening to undermine civilised life in huge swathes of the world, then governments can have no higher priority than addressing the demographic question. Tax breaks for parents may or may not be effective, but they are worth trying. As economist Philip Pilkington points out, even if we consider childbearing from a purely economic perspective, taking a woman – or one member of a couple – out of the workforce for a year or two, and creating a worker 20 years later who will work for four decades or more, must represent a good return on investment.

If pro-natalist policies can fix our demographic problems and assist populations to reproduce themselves, the wins will go far beyond a fertility uptick. There's evidence that stable and larger families are good for everything from mental health, to law and order, to lower emissions.[57] Even where pro-natal policies are seen to have only a temporary impact on fertility rates, they are effective in lowering child poverty.[58]

In most cases government action is necessary, but it is not sufficient. It can nudge fertility rates up, but it cannot move them anything like enough to return a country with a fertility rate of 1.3, say, to one of 2.3. To do this, a shift in attitudes on the part of the population is required, amounting to nothing short of a cultural revolution. It is to this that we finally now turn.

10

WHAT WE CAN DO
FOR OURSELVES

GEORGIA is a republic in the Caucasus region. It's a country slightly smaller than Scotland and a little larger than West Virginia that adopted Christianity as early as the fourth century and was absorbed into Russia in the early nineteenth century. It then became part of the Soviet Union, and received its independence when the USSR was dissolved in 1991. It is a stunning land, famed for its towering mountains (the highest is over 5,000 metres) and its ancient viticulture. But it is not just for its tourist attractions that the Republic of Georgia is of interest: its recent history contains a demographic nugget.

In the early years of this century, Georgia was suffering from the same fertility slump that afflicted much of the rest of the former Soviet Union. At not much over 1.5, its fertility rate was low for a country that was still relatively poor. Among the former Soviet republics, only the predominantly Muslim ones like neighbouring Azerbaijan and those in central Asia, which were still significantly poorer, had above-replacement fertility. In 2007, Ilia II, the Patriarch of the Georgian Orthodox Church (to which more than 80 per cent of the population belongs), said that he would personally baptise and stand as godfather to the newborns of any married couple who already had two children.

A decade later, the Patriarch was estimated to have baptised more than 30,000 babies. Births that qualified for baptism rose from about 5,000 to about 13,000 a year, and births within marriage (also a necessary qualification for the Patriarch's blessing) went up from around half to about two-thirds of total births. The country's total fertility rate shot up within a decade to replacement level, at 2.2.[1] The population of Georgia, which peaked in the early 1990s at almost 5 million, then fell in the wake of a wave of emigration, but it has now stabilised at around 3.7 million.[2]

Ilia II's initiative did not involve the government spending any money. Indeed, it did not directly involve the government at all (although the Georgian Orthodox Church is granted a 'special role' in the country's constitution and so can be thought of as a quasi-governmental body). The Church's pro-natalism was matched by subsequent state initiatives, including the extension of rights to parental leave and a larger baby bonus payment. But the particular rise among babies qualifying for the Patriarch's offer, and the timing of the leap in fertility, suggests that what happened in Georgia was more about religious culture than legal or financial incentives.

There is, of course, no guarantee that the Georgian initiative will continue to succeed – there has been a slight fall in fertility in the country over the past few years. But the total fertility rate is still close to two, and the fact that the initiative has had a material impact for more than 15 years is impressive. The country will long benefit from the additional half a child per woman achieved.

Georgia is in a relatively unusual position. The Church is not universally admired and has its liberal critics, given its conservative stance on many social issues. But it is one of the most trusted and respected institutions in the country.[3] What it has done could not be replicated exactly elsewhere. Nevertheless, it does show that there is more to boosting the fertility rate than merely relying on government actions.

CULTURAL ICONS

Churches in many other countries lack the pull of the Georgian Church. The Pope may rail against the prioritisation of pets over babies, but we do not see much impact on the fertility rate of countries where most of the population formally subscribes to Roman Catholicism. Catholic southern Europe has some of the world's smallest families, and Catholic Latin America has seen some of the fastest falls in fertility. In the unlikely circumstance that the Church of England were prepared to take a pro-natalist stand, an offer by the Archbishop of Canterbury to baptise third children is unlikely to have much impact. In fact, it is hard to find any pro-natalist statement emerging from the Church of England – consistent perhaps with the tradition of Malthus, who was, we should not forget, an Anglican clergyman.

In the US and many other countries, there is no single religious authority or established religion that would have the reach relative to the size of the country that the Georgian Orthodox Church has in Georgia. Pleas by religious leaders in Iran (who are also political leaders, given that the country is a theocracy) have done nothing to reverse the lack of children.

'Decide tonight to rid yourselves of this ominous culture of having only one or two children,' exhorts one Iranian TV cleric, who calls on his viewers to have 12 children and proclaims that 'nothing less than five is acceptable'.[4] But Iran's fertility rate remains well below two.

Nevertheless, there are institutions not directly part of the government that clearly do have cultural influence. In Britain, for example, there is the royal family. The two peaks of the post-war baby boom, in the late 1940s/early 1950s and the early to mid-1960s, coincided with Queen Elizabeth II's childbearing years (Charles and Anne were born in 1948 and 1950, Andrew and Edward in 1960 and 1964). There was no noticeable upward turn, however, in the years when princes William and Harry were born (1982 and 1984, respectively). Although it seems somewhat far-fetched to imagine people having children because the royal family are doing so, their presence in the collective imagination does not make this entirely impossible. If the UK's fertility rate has held up some-what better than that of many other European countries, the example of the royal family may have something to do with it. During the years when the current Prince and Princess of Wales's three children were born (2013 to 2018), the UK's total fertility rate was between 1.8 and 1.9, higher than it has been since (although subsequent data continue to be somewhat distorted by the pandemic).

But it is not only royal icons who can make a difference. The celebrity worlds of football and pop music came together in the marriage of David and Victoria Beckham in 1999, a marriage that has lasted and produced four children, the eldest of whom recently married at the age of 23. For sure, members of the royal family and celebrities do not face the financial and other constraints that shape the actions of the bulk of the population, but they can play their part in presenting role models for a higher-fertility society. The reverse is also true, when people like the Duke and Duchess of Sussex declare that they won't have any more children because of concerns over the planet (although, to be fair, this is after having had a respectable two).[5]

THE POLITICS AND BUSINESS OF CULTURAL INFLUENCE

The interaction between politics and culture is complicated and does not necessarily work in one direction. Politics is not always 'downstream' from culture, but sometimes helps create it. In 1983, more than a decade and a half after homosexuality was legalised, only 17 per cent of the British public thought that it was never wrong. It took another 15 years for that figure to approach 50 per cent.[6] There was half a century between the last hanging in Britain (1964) and opinion polls showing that most of the population opposed capital punishment.[7] These were cases where political positions were 'ahead' of cultural attitudes, with the result that legislation was passed by Members of Parliament who were more liberal than the general public. The public eventually caught up. So while culture is the critical ingredient in determining a country's fertility rate, we should not assume that it is free from influence by the world of politics.

Governments can and do influence national culture, beyond legislating and directly introducing pro-natal policies. In the UK a 'Behavioural Insights Team' was set up by the government in 2010, which came to be known as the 'nudge unit'.[8] It was particularly active during the Covid pandemic, encouraging certain precautionary actions on the part of the public. But even before the nudge unit's creation, the government was instituting policies designed to promote certain activities and behaviours without making them mandatory. An example is the automatic enrolment of workers in a pension scheme; another, similarly, is the assumption of consent to organ donation, but with an option to refuse this. It used to be the case that only 38 per cent of people explicitly opted in to donate organs. Now, where an implicit decision not to opt out has been taken, families consent to organ donation in 66 per cent of cases.[9]

Nudging is more about creating or influencing the social climate rather than making changes to legislation. In the UK, there could be room in the educational curriculum for issues around having children to be addressed. Sex education (now incorporated into 'personal, social, health and economic education' in the UK) has traditionally focused on preventing teenage pregnancies. It has been highly successful at this: between 2011 and 2021, conceptions among the under-16s in England and Wales fell by two-thirds, and among the under-18s by more than a half.[10] This has been in line with explicit government policy.[11] The teenage birth rate in the US too has fallen dramatically in recent years, a drop attributed to the educational efforts of governmental and non-governmental organisations alike.[12] Across the EU, there has also been a long-term decline in teenage pregnancy.[13]

If government policy, and particularly sex education, can achieve this sort of result, it might also be effective in tackling misconceptions that depress a country's fertility rate. The severe decline in fertility during a woman's thirties and a less severe decline in a man's forties are not generally well known, at least not by those younger – nor are the difficulty, expense and unreliability of interventions such as IVF and egg-freezing. Better education on the ticking fertility clock would likely spur more people into earlier action. But when the head of a Cambridge college proposed educating her students on the subject, she was met by a barrage of opposition. Dorothy Byrne, president of Murray Edwards College, said she wanted to talk 'openly about fertility, in the same way it is important to be aware of the facts about contraception'. She was accused of purveying a 'narrow view of both womanhood and the intellect of her students', and would risk alienating non-binary and minority gender students.[14] So we are effectively in a situation in which assisting the young to prevent pregnancies is utterly uncontroversial, but educating them in fertility, which might help them to have children more easily, is denounced. This is where government intervention could potentially affect the social climate without involving spending or legislation.

There is a role for companies too. Apart from their policies on parental leave and pay, which often go beyond the statutory minimum, they could think about everything from product design and advertising to homeworking in the context of its influence on the country's fertility rate. Capitalism (and every other known economic system) relies on one generation following another, and is negatively impacted if each cohort is smaller than the last. You might say that this is a social problem and that the actions of any particular company will not be significant. Yet in other fields, companies are prepared to adopt policies that have explicitly social goals. No individual company's emissions, for example, will make a significant difference to global warming, yet many large companies have stated goals on reducing their harm to the environment. When George Floyd was killed by police in Minneapolis in 2020, corporations from Japan to Ireland felt the need to express their solidarity and concern, and in many cases to make donations to Black Lives Matter or related causes.[15] If we live in an era in which corporations can respond to climate change and to racial discrimination in other countries, it should not be beyond imagining that they could play a role in combating the demographic emergency, which will very soon start directly hitting their bottom lines.

Our cultural personalities and institutions can play a part too. Great artists from Titian to Lucian Freud have had multiple offspring without it apparently cramping their style. J. S. Bach had no fewer than 20 children (born of two wives) without it seeming to affect the stellar quality or prolific quantity of his output. But leading British artist Tracey Emin insists that having children would have diminished rather than enhanced her creativity: 'Having children and being a mother... It would be a compromise to be an artist at the same time.' As Emin went on to say: 'There are good artists that have children. Of course there are. They are called men. It's hard for women. It's really difficult, they are emotionally torn. It's hard enough for me with my cat.'[16] Rachel Ruysch, the great Dutch still-life painter of the late seventeenth and early eighteenth centuries, with her prolific output and ten births, might have disagreed. So might have Clara Schumann, perhaps the greatest female composer of all time, with eight children and an exceptionally busy performing career. The recently rediscovered and widely acclaimed African American composer Florence Price, mother of two, might likewise have dissented from Emin's binary choice of motherhood or creativity. So too might the leading female impressionist painter Berthe Morisot, whose daughter was her muse and frequent model. Mary Shelley managed to produce four children as well as *Frankenstein*. Victoria Beckham has actively pursued her career as fashion designer, singer and television personality while bearing and rearing four children.

For some, fathers as well as mothers, children are a creative inspiration rather than a distraction. 'I actually found having a child was an enormous boost to my creative energy. All those naysayers and worrying folk who had warned me that motherhood would "end my career" seemed to have got it wrong,' comments one female writer.[17]

Culture, like business, depends on new blood, new ideas and the creativity of youth. Ageing and shrinking populations will diminish our cultural life, just as they will everything else. The cultural industry might want to consider its responsibilities to itself as well as towards the wider society when it divorces itself from childbearing and rails against the influence of the notorious 'pram in the hall', a symbol for the supposedly depressing effect parenthood has on artistic creativity.

FAITH AND FAMILY

As we have seen, the greatest factor working against a vortex of low fertility is religion. It provides, at least in the case of the Abrahamic faiths, an ideological set of reasons and practices that support the idea and reality of people having children. In many countries on the path to development, it seems that religion is the key to preventing their fertility rates from plummeting. And in cases of religiosity, whether Christian, Jewish or sometimes Muslim, high fertility stands out against a background of secular societies in which having children is a low priority.

These religions are generally pro-natalist in their teachings. In the Bible both Adam and Noah are commanded to be fruitful and multiply explicitly on two occasions. Despite the traditions of celibacy and monasticism in Christianity, families and marriage are celebrated. The Qur'an is less explicitly pro-natalist than the Bible, although it condemns infanticide driven by poverty and explicitly condemns the killing of daughters.[18] There are Hadiths, sayings of the Prophet recorded outside the Qur'an, which suggest that Muhammad called for people to have many children.[19]

Jews, Christians and Muslims have interpreted their texts in various ways, some allowing and some forbidding contraception under different circumstances, some permitting abortion under certain conditions, and others condemning it in all cases.[20] Catholicism has been most hard-line on banning both contraception and abortion. Islam has been particularly flexible in practice. A good example is the stance of the mullahs running the Islamic Republic of Iran. Immediately after the revolution in 1979, they shut down the family-planning programme of the previous regime, but when around a decade later they became concerned about a population explosion, they initiated a new programme that was extremely successful in reversing course and saw fertility rates tumble.[21] A subsequent change of direction has not been so successful, showing that it is much easier for governments to help bring the fertility rate down than to increase it. Iran's fertility rate remains well below replacement level and its population is ageing fast.

The teachings on procreation in other major world religions, such as Hinduism and Buddhism, are less clearly pro-natalist. Hinduism does not restrict the use of contraception.[22] Where Buddhism has preached larger families, it has tended to be in situations of ethnic conflict with non-Buddhist peoples, as a form of 'demographic engineering'.[23]

It is notable that in many societies where some form of Buddhism has been prominent, the number of children born per woman has fallen with particular rapidity as the country has modernised, and this might be because of the lack of a countervailing religious influence promoting fertility that exists where Christianity, Judaism or Islam prevail. Countries like China, Japan and Thailand are examples of this, the last seeing low fertility long before it reached anything like first-world levels of income, education or urbanisation. And we can find similar effects in predominantly Hindu India where, in some parts of the country such as West Bengal, low fertility has raced ahead of the economic and social development it was supposed to have accompanied. Again, the absence of Abrahamic religious pro-natalism influencing most of the population may be part of the explanation.

In low-fertility East Asia, it is notable that the Philippines, one of only two majority-Christian countries in the region, has maintained a significantly higher fertility rate than its neighbours. Today, the Catholic Philippines has a fertility rate about twice that of Thailand, despite being only slightly poorer. The other East Asian majority-Christian country, Timor-Leste, has a total fertility rate of above three, by far the highest in East and South East Asia. (On the other hand, Muslim Indonesia, from which Timor-Leste broke away, has maintained a fertility rate of around 2.2, similar to the level in Buddhist Myanmar, despite its people being three or four times wealthier.[24]) Where Muslims live alongside followers of non-Abrahamic faiths, such as in Malaysia, India and Sri Lanka, their fertility and growth rates are invariably higher than those of their Buddhist and Hindu neighbours.[25]

The religious attitude to procreation is useful and interesting to know, of course, but it is not clear what the implications are when it comes to doing something about the demographic crisis. Mass religious conversion is unlikely, and the high-fertility sects are only effective at growing to significant size and making a difference to overall fertility if they can retain their young within the fold, one generation after another. But to do this they need to put up barriers to the external world. The Amish and Hutterites may think they have the key to heaven. The Haredim may believe that their approach to Judaism is the only authentic one. But for the most part they are reluctant to go forth and draw in others to their creed for fear of infection from the big bad world. And even if they could undertake mass conversions, and even if this were the only way for the world to get back to higher fertility rates, the result would be a strange and fragmented set of societies. Religious groups which reach out to the world find their fertility rate converging with that of the surrounding society, as the Mormons have discovered. Without at least a moderately liberal overlay, it is hard to see a country made up of isolated sects opposed to the modern world being anything close to what we would recognise as functional.

It may be, as I have suggested, that humanity needs to go through a bottleneck during which those people die out who are culturally or genetically of a liberal disposition and refuse to have children. But we should do our best to avoid this, if at all possible, since neither the process nor the end point are likely to be agreeable. The world that would emerge from such a bottleneck would be unrecognisable from today's, and not in a way that liberals would like. A narrowing of horizons, particularly for women, and the return of patriarchy with a vengeance would be the result not of pro-natalism but of its failure.

A ROLE FOR ALL OF US

In the final analysis, whatever the social context and norms, and whatever the social implications, having a child is a personal matter and usually a personal choice. This means that it is up to every one of us who is potentially able to have a child to consider this, and weigh up the options. But people of childbearing age are only a relatively small part of the population. Age alone rules out many adults in countries with the kind of population pyramids we see in much of the developed world. Some are too old to have children; some too young. Others cannot, or for their own reasons do not wish to, have children. But this does not mean there is nothing they can do. Collectively, we shape the atmosphere and culture. We can all be kind to pregnant women, giving up our seats on the train or bus. We can all make way for someone pushing a pram. We can all help out when a colleague has a childcare crisis without resentfully reflecting on how someone else's childbearing choices end up impinging on our own time: that child will be paying your pension and may be caring for you when you are old. We can make sure not to be the sort of landlord who says 'no children', as a survey found nearly a quarter offering property for rent in the UK do, making the lives of parents needing to rent particularly difficult.[26]

We can all speak up against the wave of gloomy anti-natalism that threatens to swamp the culture. If people do not or cannot have children themselves, they can be good and caring friends, neighbours and family members, making the lives of parents torn between childcare and work that little bit easier.

We can all become advocates for pro-natalism in our own way. My son, for example, who does not necessarily share my outlook but is very fond of children and hopes to have some of his own before too long, enquired within months of joining the firm where he works about making the paternal leave more generous and more equal with maternal leave. There was a change in policy and his preparedness to meet the head of the firm and discuss the matter with her may have made a difference.

The role of grandparents is essential. In the course of writing this book I was fortunate enough to become a grandparent twice over when both my daughters had babies within a few weeks of each other. The book would have been written much faster if I, along with my wife, had not been spending quite a lot of time supporting the new parents in their joyous but daunting role, from ferrying them to prenatal appointments to taking them to the hospital for the delivery, to cooking meals and offering babysitting services to allow them to get a few hours of precious sleep after interrupted nights. Our role as grandparents will evolve as our grandsons grow and are, we hope, joined by siblings, but our own parents set us a sterling example of what a difference grandparents can make. There is solid research supporting the hypothesis that the involvement of grandparents has an impact on the fertility intentions of women.[27] And more anecdotally, one Israeli academic, trying to explain the country's surprisingly high fertility, said to me: 'This country runs on grandparents. The whole thing would be impossible without them.' The presence of grandmothers has also traditionally reduced infant mortality as new mothers benefit from the wisdom, experience and help of their own mothers.[28] That role now needs to become one of providing the incentives and potential not for lower mortality but for higher fertility, and it can be shared by grandfathers as well as grandmothers.

Then there is the special responsibility of men. We have already seen that the sharing of household chores, including childcare, is positively associated with higher fertility rates. Everyone from husbands and male partners to government ministers needs to bear in mind that while women have the biological responsibility of bearing children, more women will be more likely to have more children if the child-rearing responsibilities are more equally shared. Patriarchal attitudes in the home and in the workplace are inimical to childbearing in modern societies.

In a nutshell, modern societies are trying to balance two potentially contradictory things: on the one hand the education of women and their full participation in the workforce and at every level in society, and on the other the unchanging biological reality of birthing and all that it means. We are not going to compromise on women's rights. Either we must reconcile these with biology, or we are doomed to demographic Armageddon. We need feminists and environmentalists on board, as well as more socially conservative types. The various national-conservative parties and right-wing populist factions around the world are fundamentally pro-natalist. But the left too needs to get in touch with its pro-natalist roots, which go all the way back to Marx's opposition to Malthus. And even those who fundamentally hate the West for its sins of historical colonialism and current racism need to understand that long gone are the days when pro-natalism was a concern for whites only. Koreans and Japanese, Jamaicans and African Americans, will all disappear in due course if their current fertility rates persist, with an incalculable loss to the richness of human cultural variety. It will be a huge step forward when a belief that we need more children spans the political spectrum.

The first step, as always, is to understand the data, both the current numbers and their historical context and direction of travel. The second step is to acknowledge we have a problem. The third is to figure out a solution. I do not have all the answers, and the solutions to perennial low fertility will vary over time and in different places. What works in one country at one time will not work in another country, or in the same country at a later date. Bold experimentation will be required. But we must try.

THE MAKING OF A PRO-NATAL CULTURE AND THE SAVING OF HUMANITY

Every person we have ever loved or cared about, every genius whose work we have marvelled at, every great person whose actions and words have inspired us, every one of these, like us, has come into being only because of procreation. Without humanity the world would continue to spin on its axis but there would be no art, no culture, no music, no politics, no great cities, nor any extraordinary scientific innovations. Some might prefer such a world, devoid of human influence, and devoid of humans. For those of us who would not, it is incumbent upon us to resurrect a pro-natal culture, something that was once innate in humans but is now in desperate need of being promoted.

Humanity must look itself in the face and realise that it is staring into a demographic abyss. The natural, unconstrained and uncontrolled reproduction that has marked almost all of human history has been upended by urbanisation, education, rising living standards, the mastering of technology for controlling fertility, and the allure and excitement of many alternative projects. This was at first the preserve of a small, wealthy global minority, but it has now spread to almost every country on the planet. Now we must invent ways of thinking and living that include freedom and opportunity but that place procreation at their heart. *How* we will do that will be through a mix of policy and practice, advocacy, exhortation, role-modelling, cultural influence and goodness knows what else: this book by no means contains all the answers. *That* we must do it is I hope now beyond question.

NOTES

1. The Infertile Crescent – the Looming Demographic Armageddon

1 *Daily Telegraph*, 3rd February 2023, https://www.telegraph.co.uk/world-news/2023/02/03/tactics-behind-russias-human-wave-attacks-bakhmut/; ABC News [Australia], 24th February 2021, https://www.abc.net.au/news/2021-09-25/uk-faces-fuel-shortages-and-lack-of-truck-drivers/100491042; CH Aviation, 15th September 2022, https://www.ch-aviation.com/portal/news/119477-staff-shortage-continues-to-disrupt-amsterdam-schiphol; *South China Morning Post*, 13th January 2022, https://shorturl.at/cpRY1 (impressions: 22nd March 2024).

2 UN Population Division, https://population.un.org/wpp2019/ (impression: 13th March 2023).

3 For a more detailed discussion of the meaning of fertility rates and birth rates, see Paul Morland, *The Human Tide: How Population Shaped the Modern World*, London, John Murray, 2019.

4 In demographic terms, a cohort is a group of people born at a similar time. So baby-boomers are those born in the couple of decades after the end of the Second World War. They were once the young generation; they are now an ageing generation, but they are always the same cohort.

5 BBC, 18th January 2023, https://www.bbc.com/future/article/20230118-is-chinas-population-decline-surprising (impression: 12th March 2024).

6 UN Population Division, op. cit.

7 Throughout this book I use the term 'family size' to stand for general fertility, not for the fertility of those who actually have children. The latter use of the term, which is not my usage but is current, does not look at the fertility rate of all women but of those who actually have children, thus stripping out the childless.

8 UCL, 14th February 2022, https://blogs.ucl.ac.uk/assa/2022/02/14/the-new-sandwich-generation-in-urban-china/ (impression: 29th August 2023).

9 UN Population Division, op. cit.

10 Gov.uk, https://ukhsa.blog.gov.uk/2019/01/29/ageing-and-health-expenditure/; UN Population Division, op. cit. (impression: 16th April 2024)

11 World Population Review, https://worldpopulationreview.com/country-rankings/debt-to-gdp-ratio-by-country (impression: 18th September 2023).

12 *Economist*, 6th May 2023, p. 67.

13 D. Spears et al., 'Long-term Population Projections: Scenarios of Low or Rebounding Fertility', 2023, https://papers.ssrn.com/sol3/papers.cfm?abstract_id=4534047 (impression: 29th November 2023).

14 World Economic Forum, 19th October 2021, https://www.weforum.org/agenda/2021/10/human-impact-earth-planet-change-development/ (impression: 18th April 2023).

15 BBC, 29th August 2018, https://www.bbc.co.uk/news/world-europe-45342721; *Guardian*, 16th March 2023, https://www.theguardian.com/world/2023/mar/16/emmanuel-macron-uses-special-powers-to-force-pension-reform-france (impressions: 14th April 2023).

16 The data here and given below regarding dependency ratios come from UN Population Division, op. cit.

17 The *dependency ratio* is the ratio of all those too old or too young to work to all those of working age. Having more children will worsen the dependency ratio, but it is the only way in the long term – short of mass immigration, discussed in Chapter 7 – to improve the *old age dependency ratio*. Children require resources – food, housing, education – and do not contribute to the economy, so they do create a strain on it. But this should be thought of as an investment with a return when they enter the workplace.

18 UN Population Division, op. cit.

19 *Economist*, 3rd June 2023, pp. 16–18.

20 *New York Times*, 15th November 2021, https://www.nytimes. com/2021/11/15/world/asia/adult-diapers-japan.html (impression: 18th April 2023). This has been called into question by the BBC's *More or Less* programme.

21 CNBC, 7th December 2021, https://www.cnbc.com/2021/12/07/ elon-musk-civilization-will-crumble-if-we-dont-have-more-children.html (impression: 7th August 2023).

22 Euronews, 23rd June 2023, https://www.euronews.com/2023/06/23/ german-lawmakers-approve-a-plan-to-attract-skilled-workers-to-plug-the-countrys-labor-gap (impression: 7th August 2023).

23 Bloomberg, 29th March 2023, https://www.bloomberg.com/news/ articles/2023-03-29/japan-to-face-11-million-worker-shortfall-by-2040-study-finds#xj4y7vzkg (impression: 7th August 2023).

24 Insider, 1st February 2023, https://www.businessinsider.com/china-shrinking-population-worker-labor-shortage-grim-omen-global-economy-2023-2?r=US&IR=T (impression: 7th August 2023).

25 East Asia Forum, 19th March 2023, https://www.eastasiaforum. org/2023/03/19/demography-poses-no-imminent-threat-to-chinas-economic-modernisation/ (impression: 8th September 2023).

26 *New York Times*, 30th November 2017, https://www.nytimes. com/2017/11/30/world/asia/japan-lonely-deaths-the-end.html (impression: 16th April 2024).

27 Statista, https://www.statista.com/statistics/1113954/china-tertiary-education-college-university-enrollment-rate/ (impression: 8th September 2023).

28 Jesus Fernandez Villa-Verde, Ventura Gustavo and Wen Yao, 'The Wealth of Working Nations', 19th November 2023, https://www. sas.upenn.edu/~jesusfv/Wealth_Working_Nations.pdf (impression: 1st December 2023).

29 Population Matters, 24th May 2023, https://populationmatters.org/ news/2023/05/pronatalism-in-the-uk/ (impression: 9th August 2023).

30 William Petersen, 'John Maynard Keynes's Theories of Population and the Concept of "Optimum"', *Population Studies*, 8(3), 1955, pp. 228–46.

31 The measurement of the total fertility rate (expected children per woman) is newer than that of the birth rate (births relative to the size of the population as a whole) and did not exist in the interwar period, but has been retrospectively calculated.

32 ONS, https://www.ons.gov.uk/peoplepopulationandcommunity/ birthsdeathsandmarriages/livebirths/bulletins/birthsummarytables englandandwales/2021 (impression: 7th August 2023).

33 ONS, https://www.ons.gov.uk/peoplepopulationandcommunity/ birthsdeathsandmarriages/conceptionandfertilityrates/adhocs/14 218estimatedagespecificandtotalfertilityratesforukbornandnonuk bornwomenlivingintheukscotlandandnorthernireland (impression: 7th August 2023).

34 US Census, 6th April 2022, https://www.census.gov/library/ stories/2022/04/fertility-rates-declined-for-younger-women-increased-for-older-women.html (impression: 9th August 2023).

35 UN, https://w3.unece.org/PXWeb/en/Table?IndicatorCode=34; *Los Angeles Times*, 6th May 2022, https://www.latimes.com/world-nation/story/2022-05-06/motherhood-deferred-us-median-age-for-giving-birth-hits-30 (impressions: 7th August 2023).

36 OnePoll, 31st July 2023, https://mr.onepoll.com/attitudes-to-parenthood/ (impression: 7th August 2023).

37 Relevant, 28th July 2023, https://relevantmagazine.com/life5/one-in-four-gen-z-and-millennials-say-no-to-ever-having-a-baby/ (impression: 7th August 2023).

38 Forbes, 20th June 2022, https://www.forbes.com/sites/christinecarter/ 2022/06/20/gen-z-women-postpone-motherhood-because-of-the-challenges-working-millennial-moms-encounter/?sh=3a66c1f82b90 (impression: 7th August 2023).

39 *Guardian*, 23rd April 2021, https://www.theguardian.com/society/ 2021/apr/23/i-had-second-thoughts-the-gen-z-ers-choosing-not-to-have-children (impression: 7th August 2023).

40 ONS, https://www.ons.gov.uk/peoplepopulationandcommunity/ birthsdeathsandmarriages/conceptionandfertilityrates/bulletins/ childbearingforwomenbornindifferentyearsenglandandwales/2020 (impression: 14th November 2023).

41 British Fertility Society, https://www.britishfertilitysociety.org.uk/

fei/at-what-age-does-fertility-begin-to-decrease/ (impression: 14th
November 2023).

42 Paul Morland, *Tomorrow's People: The Future of Humanity in Ten Numbers*, London, Picador, 2022, pp. 249–53.

43 Paul Morland and Philip Pilkington, 'Migration, Stagnation, or Procreation: Quantifying the Demographic Trilemma', ARC Research, October 2023, https://www.arc-research.org/research-papers/the-demographic-trilemma (impression: 14th November 2023).

44 See Charles Goodhart and Manoj Pradhan, *The Great Demographic Reversal: Ageing Societies, Waning Inequality, and the Inflation Revival*, Cham, Switzerland, Palgrave Macmillan, 2020.

45 Buildings and Cities, 9th February 2021, https://www.buildingsandcities.org/insights/commentaries/sustainability-single-households.html (impression: 29th August 2023).

46 IMF, https://www.imf.org/external/datamapper/exp@FPP/USA/FRA/JPN/GBR/SWE/ESP/ITA/ZAF/IND (impression: 8th August 2023).

47 IMF, https://www.imf.org/external/datamapper/CG_DEBT_GDD@GDD/CHN/FRA/DEU/ITA/JPN/GBR/USA (impression: 8th August 2023).

48 World Government Bonds, http://www.worldgovernmentbonds.com/country/japan/ (impression: 8th August 2023).

49 Macrotrends, https://www.macrotrends.net/2593/nikkei-225-index-historical-chart-data (impression: 8th August 2023).

50 Nippon.com, 10th July 2023, https://www.nippon.com/en/japan-data/h01720/ (impression: 8th August 2023).

51 Trading Economics, https://tradingeconomics.com/united-kingdom/government-bond-yield (impression: 8th August 2023).

52 Reuters, 2nd August 2023, https://www.reuters.com/markets/us/fitch-cuts-us-governments-aaa-credit-rating-by-one-notch-2023-08-01/ (impression: 8th August 2023).

53 *Financial Times*, 17th May 2023, https://www.ft.com/content/f434c586-db1f-4d81-8b29-989db5c78f72 (impression: 12th September 2023).

54 Felix C. Tropf et al., 'Human Fertility, Molecular Genetics, and Natural Selection in Modern Societies', *PLOS One*, 13th June

2013; *Guardian*, 3rd June 2015, https://www.theguardian.com/science/2015/jun/03/genetics-plays-role-in-deciding-at-what-age-women-have-first-child-says-study (impressions: 8th August 2023).

55 NCSU, https://www.newsocialcovenant.co.uk/family/closing-the-birthgap/ (impression: 30th November 2023).

56 Ohio State University, 12th January 2023, https://news.osu.edu/falling-birth-rate-not-due-to-less-desire-to-have-children/ (impression: 30th November 2023).

57 YouGov, 24th June 2021, https://yougov.co.uk/society/articles/36590-one-twelve-parents-say-they-regret-having-children (impression: 30th November 2023).

2. Paths to Low Fertility

1 UK Parliament, https://www.parliament.uk/about/living-heritage/evolutionofparliament/legislativescrutiny/parliamentandireland/overview/the-great-famine/ (impression: 19th April 2023).

2 Massimo Livi-Bacci, *A Concise History of World Population*, Chichester, Wiley-Blackwell, 2012, p. 25.

3 This is the subject of my second book, *The Human Tide: How Population Shaped the Modern World*, London, John Murray, 2019.

4 UN Population Division, https://population.un.org/wpp2019/ (impression: 13th March 2023).

5 Bryan Caplan, *Selfish Reasons to Have More Kids: Why Being a Great Parent Is Less Work and More Fun than You Think*, New York, Basic Books, 2011, p. 112.

6 The Print, 28th October 2021, https://theprint.in/health/what-explains-kolkatas-falling-fertility-rate-aspiration-financial-strain-contraceptive-coverage/757667/ (impression: 18th April 2023).

7 World Health Organization, https://apps.who.int/gho/data/node.searo.NODESUBREGfertility-ETH?lang=en (impression: 18th April 2023); World Bank, https://data.worldbank.org/indicator/SP.DYN.TFRT.IN (impression: 12th March 2024).

8 John C. Caldwell, 'Toward a Restatement of Demographic Transition

Theory', *Population and Development Review*, 2(3–4), 1976, pp. 321–66.

9   World Bank, https://data.worldbank.org/indicator/NY.GDP.PCAP. CD (impression: 12th March 2024).

10 Al Jazeera, 22nd February 2023, https://www.aljazeera.com/ news/2023/2/22/tunisias-saied-says-migration-aimed-at-changing-demography (impression: 10th May 2023).

11 World Bank, https://data.worldbank.org/indicator/NY.GDP. PCAP.KD?locations=RW; World Bank, https://data.worldbank. org/indicator/SP.DYN.TFRT.IN?locations=RW (impressions: 12th May 2024).

12 BBC, 6th November 2015, https://www.bbc.co.uk/news/world-africa-34732609; Statista, https://www.statista.com/statistics/1319001/ fertility-rate-in-kenya-by-county/ (impressions: 9th May 2023).

13 World Bank, https://data.worldbank.org/indicator/SP.DYN.TFRT. IN?locations=KE (impression: 12th March 2024).

14 At purchasing power parity; World Bank, https://data.worldbank. org/indicator/NY.GDP.PCAP.PP.CD?locations=KE; World Health Organization, https://data.who.int/countries/404 (impressions: 12th March 2024).

15 Macrotrends, https://www.macrotrends.net/countries/KEN/kenya/ literacy-rate (impression: 9th May 2023).

16 World Bank, https://data.worldbank.org/indicator/SP.DYN.LE00. IN?locations=CF (impression: 12th March 2024); Macrotrends, https://www.macrotrends.net/countries/CAF/central-african-republic/literacy-rate (impression: 9th May 2023).

17 GlobalData, https://www.globaldata.com/data-insights/ macroeconomic/female-literacy-rate-in-nigeria/ (impression: 10th May 2023).

18 Ayo Stephen Adebowale, 'Ethnic Disparities in Fertility and Its Determinants in Nigeria', *Fertility Research and Practice*, 5, 2019, Article 3.

19 Countryeconomy.com, https://countryeconomy.com/demography/ religions/nigeria?year=2000 (impression: 10th May 2023).

20 The Conversation, 12th March 2023, https://theconversation.com/ nigerias-cities-are-growing-fast-family-planning-must-be-part-of-

urban-development-plans-199325 (impression: 10th May 2023). This data is now somewhat out of date but there is no reason to think that the differential has not persisted.

21 World Bank, https://data.worldbank.org/indicator/SP.DYN.LE00. IN?locations=CF (impression: 22nd March 2024).

22 World Population Review, https://worldpopulationreview.com/ world-cities/niamey-population; Macrotrends, https://www. macrotrends.net/global-metrics/cities/22007/lagos/population; World Bank, https://data.worldbank.org/indicator/SP.URB.TOTL. IN.ZS (impressions: 22nd March 2024).

23 World Population Review https://worldpopulationreview.com/country-rankings/literacy-rate-by-country (impression: 22nd March 2024).

24 *Globe and Mail*, 6th April 2017, https://www.theglobeandmail. com/news/world/africa-contraception-and-population-growth/ article34599155/ (impression: 15th May 2023).

25 *Economist*, 8th April 2023, p. 37.

26 Bright Opoku Ahinkorah et al., 'Drivers of Desire for More Children among Child-bearing Women in sub-Saharan Africa: Implications for Fertility Control', *BMC Pregnancy and Childbirth*, 20(1), 2020.

27 New Security Beat, 11th May 2015, https://www.newsecuritybeat. org/2015/05/whats-west-central-africas-youthful-demographics-high-desired-family-size/ (impression: 12th February 2023).

28 Our World in Data, https://ourworldindata.org/grapher/fertility-and-wanted-fertility (impression: 12th May 2023).

29 I showed this in my book *Tomorrow's People: The Future of Humanity in Ten Numbers*, London, Picador, 2022.

30 Ron Lesthaeghe, 'The Second Demographic Transition: A Concise Overview of Its Development', *PNAS*, 111(51), 2014, pp. 18112–5.

31 World Population Review, https://worldpopulationreview.com/ country-rankings/out-of-wedlock-births-by-country (impression: 18th September 2023).

32 Office for National Statistics, https://shorturl.at/jsBNR (impression: 12th March 2024).

33 Tomáš Sobotka, Anna Matysiak and Zusanna Brzozwska, 'Policy Responses to Low Fertility: How Effective Are They?', UNFPA, 2019, p. 13.

34 Lyman Stone, 'The Truth about Demographic Decline', Law and Liberty, 2nd January 2023, https://lawliberty.org/forum/the-truth-about-demographic-decline/ (impression: 8th September 2023).

35 World Population Review, https://worldpopulationreview.com/country-rankings/alcoholism-by-country; World Population Review, https://worldpopulationreview.com/country-rankings/drug-use-by-country (impressions: 8th September 2023).

3. Explaining Today's Low Fertility

1 Euronews, 15th June 2023, https://www.euronews.com/next/2023/06/15/sperm-counts-are-declining-scientists-believe-they-have-pinpointed-the-main-causes-why (impression: 30th November 2023).

2 NHS, https://www.nhs.uk/pregnancy/trying-for-a-baby/how-long-it-takes-to-get-pregnant/ (impression: 30th November 2023); Alison Taylor, 'ABC of Subfertility: Extent of the Problem', *British Medical Journal*, 327(7413), 2003, pp. 494–7.

3 Guillaume Blanc, 'The Cultural Origins of the Demographic Transition in France', p. 28, https://www.guillaumeblanc.com/files/theme/Blanc_secularization.pdf (impression: 8th December 2023).

4 Robert Tombs, *France 1814–1914*, London and New York, Longman, 1996, pp. 321–5.

5 Institute for Family Studies, 8th August 2022, https://ifstudies.org/blog/americas-growing-religious-secular-fertility-divide (impression: 19th April 2023).

6 Pew Research Center, 14th December 2021, https://www.pewresearch.org/religion/2021/12/14/about-three-in-ten-u-s-adults-are-now-religiously-unaffiliated/ (impression: 19th April 2023).

7 Nitzan Peri-Roem, 'Fertility Rates by Education in Britain and France: The Role of Religion', *Population*, 75(1), 2020, pp. 9–36.

8 Pablo Brañas-Garza and Shoshana Neuman, 'Is Fertility Related to Religiosity? Evidence from Spain', *Population Studies*, 60(2), 2007, pp. 219–24.

9 Barbara S. Okun, 'Religiosity and Fertility: Jews in Israel', *European Journal of Population*, 33(4), 2017, pp. 475–507.

10 Eric Kaufmann, 'Islamism, Religiosity and Fertility in the Muslim World', 2009, https://www.sneps.net/RD/uploads/1-Islamismfertilitypaper.pdf (impression: 19th April 2019).

11 Vegard Skirbekk et al., 'Is Buddhism the Low Fertility Religion of Asia?', *Demographic Research*, 32(1), 2015, pp. 1–28.

12 Sylvie Dubuc, 'Fertility and Population in the UK: Trends and Outlooks', paper presented at the Population Association of America conference, 2009.

13 Hispanic Children and Families, 6th March 2019, https://www.hispanicresearchcenter.org/research-resources/hispanic-women-are-helping-drive-the-recent-decline-in-the-us-fertility-rate/ (impression: 19th April 2023).

14 Statista, https://www.statista.com/statistics/226292/us-fertility-rates-by-race-and-ethnicity/ (impression: 19th April 2023).

15 UN Population Division, https://population.un.org/wpp2019/ (impression: 13th March 2023); World Bank, https://data.worldbank.org/indicator/SP.DYN.TFRT.IN (impression: 14th March 2024).

16 World Bank, 24th November 2015, https://blogs.worldbank.org/health/female-education-and-childbearing-closer-look-data (impression: 6th July 2023).

17 *Economist*, 8th April 2018, p. 39.

18 Brady E. Hamilton, 'Total Fertility Rates, by Maternal Educational Attainment and Race and Hispanic Origin: United States, 2019', *National Vital Statistics Report*, 70(5), 2021.

19 CPC, October 2015, http://www.cpc.ac.uk/docs/BP29_Educational_differences_in_childbearing_widen-in_Britain.pdf (impression: 19th April 2023).

20 John Ermisch, 'English Fertility Heads South: Understanding the Recent Decline', *Demographic Research*, 45, 2021, pp. 903–16.

21 Ann Berrington, 'Childlessness in the UK', in Michaela Kreyenfeld and Dirk Konietzka, *Childlessness in Europe: Contexts, Causes, and Consequences*, Berlin, Springer, 2017, pp. 57–76.

22 *Guardian*, 29th January 2013, https://www.theguardian.com/education/

datablog/2013/jan/29/how-many-men-and-women-are-studying-at-my-university (impression: 20th April 2023).

23 Phys.org, 1st August 2019, https://phys.org/news/2019-08-women-tinder-highly-men.html (impression: 19th April 2023).

24 Anna-Kristin Kuhnt, Michaela Kreyenfeld and Heike Trappe, 'Fertility Ideals of Women and Men across the Life Course', in Michaela Kreyenfeld and Dirk Konietzka, *Childlessness in Europe: Contexts, Causes, and Consequences*, Berlin, Springer, 2017, pp. 235–52.

25 OECD Family Database, https://www.oecd.org/els/family/SF_2_2-Ideal-actual-number-children.pdf (impression: 25th January 2024).

26 Institute for Family Studies, 18th November 2020, https://ifstudies.org/blog/the-conservative-fertility-advantage (impression: 19th April 2023).

27 Ibid.

28 Ibid.

29 *Guardian*, 7th September 2022, https://www.theguardian.com/lifeandstyle/2022/sep/07/having-children-may-make-you-more-conservative-study-finds (impression: 19th April 2023).

30 Tom S. Vogl and Jeremy Freese, 'Differential Fertility Makes Society More Conservative', *PNAS*, 117(14), 2020, pp. 7696–701.

31 World Bank, https://data.worldbank.org/indicator/NY.GDP.PCAP.CD; World Bank, https://data.worldbank.org/indicator/SP.DYN.TFRT.IN (impressions: 13th March 2024).

32 *Guardian*, 13th October 2021, https://www.theguardian.com/lifeandstyle/2021/oct/13/it-is-devastating-the-millennials-who-would-love-to-have-kids-but-cant-afford-a-family (impression: 19th April 2023).

33 Open Access Government, 28th March 2022, https://www.openaccessgovernment.org/women-childcare-policy-spring-budget-uk-government/132626/ (impression: 20th April 2023).

34 *i*, 15th November 2022, https://inews.co.uk/news/love-another-baby-cant-afford-brutal-childcare-costs-1971217 (impression: 20th April 2023).

35 Good to Know, 18th October 2021, https://www.goodto.com/family/babies/childcare-costs-are-why-i-cant-afford-a-second-child-624960 (impression: 20th April 2023).

36 OECD, June 2020, https://web-archive.oecd.org/2020-06-05/554683-OECD-Is-Childcare-Affordable.pdf; Euronews Next, 20th March 2022, https://www.euronews.com/next/2023/03/06/childcare-puzzle-which-countries-in-europe-have-the-highest-and-lowest-childcare-costs (impressions: 20th April 2023).

37 Adam Smith Institute, https://static1.squarespace.com/static/56eddde7 62cd9413e151ac92/t/5968e14e86e6c08c90fda56c/1500045650060/ Housing+and+fertility.pdf (impression: 20th April 2023).

38 Ibid.

39 ONS, https://www.ons.gov.uk/peoplepopulationandcommunity/ birthsdeathsandmarriages/livebirths/datasets/birthsummarytables (impression: 24th April 2023).

40 Numbeo, https://www.numbeo.com/property-investment/rankings_ by_country.jsp (impression: 20th April 2023).

41 *Washington Post*, 2nd December 2022, https://www.washingtonpost. com/climate-environment/2022/12/02/climate-kids/ (impression: 19th April 2023).

42 *Guardian*, 27th November 2020, https://www.theguardian.com/ environment/2020/nov/27/climate-apocalypse-fears-stopping-people-having-children-study (impression: 20th April 2023).

43 *News International*, 23rd October 2022, https://www.thenews.com. pk/latest/1002741-meghan-markle-prince-harry-not-considering-a-third-child-royal-expert-believes (impression: 19th April 2023).

44 *Guardian*, 27th February 2019, https://www.theguardian.com/ environment/shortcuts/2019/feb/27/is-alexandria-ocasio-cortez-right-to-ask-if-the-climate-means-we-should-have-fewer-children (impression: 19th April 2023).

45 *Washington Post*, op. cit.

46 The Birthstrike Movement, https://birthstrikemovement.org/ (impression: 19th April 2023).

47 *Daily Mail*, 29th March 2016, https://www.dailymail.co.uk/femail/ article-3513800/Holly-Brockwell-reveals-happiness-wins-four-year-battle-sterilised-Morning.html (impression: 8th June 2023).

48 Bryan Caplan, *Selfish Reasons to Have More Kids: Why Being a Great Parent Is Less Work and More Fun than You Think*, New York, Basic Books, 2011, p. 134.

49 Therese Hesketh, Li Lu and Zhu Wei Xing, 'The Consequences of Son Preference and Sex-selective Abortion in China and Other Asian Countries', *Canadian Medical Association Journal*, 183(12), 2011, pp. 1374–7.

50 *Hankyoreh*, 7th January 2020, https://english.hani.co.kr/arti/english_edition/e_national/923529.html; Statista, https://www.statista.com/statistics/455905/urbanization-in-south-korea/ (impressions: 5th July 2023).

51 World Bank, https://data.worldbank.org/indicator/NY.GDP.PCAP.CD?locations=KR; World Bank, https://data.worldbank.org/indicator/NY.GDP.PCAP.CD?locations=JP (impressions: 14th March 2024).

52 Statista, https://www.statista.com/statistics/629032/south-korea-university-enrollment-rate/ (impression: 5th July 2023).

53 Statista, https://www.statista.com/statistics/1378142/south-korea-daily-time-spent-on-house-chores-by-gender/ (impression: 5th July 2023).

54 OECD, https://www.oecd.org/els/family/SF_2_4_Share_births_outside_marriage.pdf (impression: 4th July 2023).

55 Insider, 7th July 2021, https://www.insider.com/people-in-seoul-arent-having-sex-study-2021-7 (impression: 2nd August 2023).

56 Korea.net, https://www.korea.net/AboutKorea/Korean-Life/Religion (impression: 5th July 2023).

57 *New York Times*, 16th May 2023, https://www.nytimes.com/2023/05/16/world/asia/korea-no-kids-zones.html (impression: 5th July 2023).

4. Where Fertility Persists

1 Yale University, Genocide Studies Program, https://gsp.yale.edu/case-studies/indonesia (impression: 19th May 2023).

2 World Bank, https://data.worldbank.org/indicator/NY.GDP.PCAP.KN?locations=ID (impression: 19th May 2023).

3 UNESCO, 26th February 2016, https://uil.unesco.org/case-study/effective-practices-database-litbase-0/akrab-literacy-creates-power-indonesia; GlobalData, https://www.globaldata.com/data-insights/macroeconomic/literacy-rate-in-indonesia/ (impressions: 19th May 2023).

4   UNESCO, https://gpseducation.oecd.org/CountryProfile?primaryCountry=IDN&treshold=10&topic=EO (impression: 19th May 2023).

5   World Bank, https://data.worldbank.org/indicator/SP.URB.TOTL?locations=ID (impression: 14th March 2024).

6   Mohamad Dziqie Aulia Al Farauqi and M. Najeri Al Syahrin, 'Governmentality, the Discourse, and Indonesia's Family Planning Program', https://eudl.eu/pdf/10.4108/eai.18-11-2020.2311626 (impression: 22nd May 2023).

7   For the establishment of the programme, see T. H. Reese, 'The Indonesian National Family Planning Program', *Bulletin of Indonesian Economic Studies*, 11(3), 1975, pp. 104–16.

8   T. H. Hull, V. J. Hull and M. Singarimbun, 'Indonesia's Family Planning Story: Success and Challenge', *Population Bulletin*, 32(6), 1977, pp. 1–52.

9   World Bank, https://data.worldbank.org/indicator/NY.GDP.MKTP.KD.ZG?locations=ID; World Bank, https://data.worldbank.org/indicator/NY.GDP.MKTP.KD.ZG?locations=TH (impressions: 14th March 2024).

10 WorldData.info, https://www.worlddata.info/country-comparison.php?country1=IDN&country2=THA#economy (impression: 21st May 20223).

11 Rainer Kotschy, Patricio Suarez Urtaza and Uwe Sunde, 'The Demographic Dividend is More than an Education Dividend', *PNAS*, 117(42), 2020, pp. 25982–4.

12 Kristin Snopkowski and James Joseph Nelson, 'Fertility Intentions and Outcomes in Indonesia: Evolutionary Perspectives on Sexual Conflict', *Evolutionary Human Sciences*, 3, 2021.

13 Ratna Dwi Wulandari, Agung Dwi Laksono and Ratu Matahari, 'The Barrier to Contraceptive Use among Multiparous Women in Indonesia', *Indian Journal of Community Medicine*, 46(3), 2021, pp. 479–83.

14 Countryeconomy.com, https://countryeconomy.com/countries/compare/india/indonesia?sc=XE34; NationMaster, https://

NOTES

www.nationmaster.com/country-info/compare/India/Indonesia/ Education; World Bank, https://data.worldbank.org/indicator/ SP.URB.TOTL.IN.ZS (impressions: 21st May 2023).

15 Pew Research Center, 21st November 2021, https://www. pewresearch.org/religion/2021/09/21/religious-composition-of-india/ (impression: 21st May 2023).

16 Homegrown, 8th March 2022, https://homegrown.co.in/home grown-creators/i-don-t-want-kids-that-s-okay-indian-women-talk-about-their-views-on-motherhood (impression: 21st May 2023).

17 GlobalDataLab, https://globaldatalab.org/areadata/table/tfr/IDN/ (impression: 22nd May 2023).

18 India Budget, https://www.indiabudget.gov.in/economicsurvey/doc/ stat/tab818.pdf (impression: 22nd May 2022).

19 Indian Ministry of Labour and Employment, 7th April 2022, https:// pib.gov.in/PressReleasePage.aspx?PRID=1814543 (impression: 13th November 2023).

20 Ibid.

21 *Buenos Aires Times*, 28th April 2022, https://www.batimes.com.ar/ news/argentina/average-argentine-woman-now-gives-birth-to-less-than-two-children.phtml (impression: 23rd May 2023).

22 BBC, 5th January 2022, https://www.bbc.co.uk/news/world-europe-59884801 (impression: 23rd May 2023).

23 BBC, 12th May 2023, https://www.bbc.co.uk/news/world-europe-65572153 (impression: 24th May 2023).

24 Cultural Atlas, 2018, https://culturalatlas.sbs.com.au/argentine-culture/argentine-culture-religion (impression: 23rd May 2023).

25 *Washington Post*, 18th January 2021, https://www.washingtonpost. com/politics/2021/01/18/argentina-legalized-abortion-heres-how-it-happened-what-it-means-latin-america/ (impression: 24th May 2023).

26 Medium, 7th June 2019, https://medium.com/@sanjayaben/facts-myths-about-sri-lankan-population-growth-f4782c23beb5 (impression: 24th May 2023).

27 Deborah S. DeGraff and K. A. P. Siddhisena, 'Unmet Need for Family Planning in Sri Lanka: Low Enough or Still an Issue?',

International Perspectives on Sexual and Reproductive Health, 41(4), 2015, p. 200.

28 *Jerusalem Post*, 22nd January 2024, https://www.jpost.com/health-and-wellness/article-783142 (impression: 25th January 2024).

29 World Bank, https://data.worldbank.org/indicator/NY.GDP.PCAP. CD (impression: 14th March 2024).

30 OECD, https://data.oecd.org/eduatt/population-with-tertiary-education.htm (impression: 5th June 2023).

31 NationMaster, https://www.nationmaster.com/country-info/stats/ Industry/Patent-applications/Residents/Per-capita (impression: 5th June 2023).

32 World Bank, https://data.worldbank.org/indicator/SP.URB.TOTL. IN.ZS (impression: 14th March 2024).

33 UN, https://www.un.org/unispal/document/auto-insert-210930/ (impression: 6th June 2023).

34 S. DellaPergola and J. Even, eds, *Papers in Jewish Demography*, Jerusalem, Hebrew University Press, 1997, pp. 11–33.

35 Philippe Fargues, 'Protracted National Conflict and Fertility Change: Palestinians and Israelis in the Twentieth Century', *Population and Development Review*, 23(6), 2000, p. 447.

36 Ibid., p. 448.

37 Kai Bird, *Crossing the Mandelbaum Gate: Coming of Age between the Arabs and Israelis, 1956–1978*, London, New York, Scribner, 2010, p. 219.

38 Paul Morland, *Demographic Engineering: Population Strategies in Ethnic Conflict*, Farnham, Ashgate, 2014, pp. 114–21.

39 Ibid., p. 122.

40 Israel Central Bureau of Statistics, https://www.cbs.gov.il/en/ publications/pages/2023/fertility-of-jewish-and-other-women-in-israel-by-level-of-religiosity-1979%E2%80%932022.aspx (impression: 14th March 2024).

41 CityPopulation, https://www.citypopulation.de/en/israel/admin/ west_bank/3797__modiin_illit/ (impression: 6th June 2023).

42 CityPopulation, https://www.citypopulation.de/en/israel/telaviv/ admin/0681__givat_shemuel/ (impression: 6th June 2023).

43 Israel Central Bureau of Statistics, op. cit.

44 Fargues, op. cit., p. 460.

45 Dov Chernichovsky et al., *The Health of the Israeli Arab Population*, Jerusalem, Taub Center, 2017, pp. 16, 17.

46 Israel Central Bureau of Statistics, op. cit.

47 J. Anson and A. Meir, 'Religiosity, Nationalism and Fertility in Israel', *European Journal of Population*, 12(1), 1996, pp. 1–25. The data on this are now fairly old and I have found nothing more recent in English.

48 OECD, https://www.oecd-ilibrary.org/sites/c63e99a9-en/index. html?itemId=/content/component/c63e99a9-en (impression: 7th June 2023).

49 Taub Center, December 2018, https://www.taubcenter.org.il/en/ research/israels-exceptional-fertility/ (impression: 7th June 2023).

50 OECD, https://www.oecd-ilibrary.org/sites/c63e99a9-en/index. html?itemId=/content/component/c63e99a9-en (impression: 7th June 2023).

51 Eurostat, 17th July 2020, https://ec.europa.eu/eurostat/web/products-eurostat-news/-/ddn-20200717-1 (impression: 7th June 2023).

52 OECD, https://www.oecd.org/els/family/SF_2_4_Share_births_ outside_marriage.pdf (impression: 7th June 2023).

53 Pew Research Center, 11th May 2021, https://www.pewresearch. org/religion/2021/05/11/jewish-demographics/ (impression: 9th June 2023).

54 *Jewish Chronicle*, 8th April 2022, https://www.thejc.com/lets-talk/ all/the-riddle-of-modern-israel%27s-remarkably-high-birth-rates-2d3Ch8U5grh4kAYH42j7sR (impression: 9th June 2023).

55 For Hamas, see UN, https://www.un.org/unispal/document/auto-insert-182893/ (impression: 9th June 2023). For Iran, see *Atlantic*, 15th July 2022, https://www.theatlantic.com/ideas/archive/2022/07/ joe-biden-middle-east-israel-iran/670530/ (impression: 9th June 2023).

56 Jewish Virtual Library, https://www.jewishvirtuallibrary.org/jewish-population-of-the-world (impression: 11th June 2023).

57 Morland, 2014, op. cit., p. 124.

58 UN Population Division, https://population.un.org/wpp2019/ (impression: 13th March 2023).

59 Morland, 2014, op. cit., p. 129.

60 Ibid.

61 World Population Review, https://worldpopulationreview.com/country-rankings/maternity-leave-by-country; Lexology, 5th December 2021, https://www.lexology.com/library/detail.aspx?g=be7affc8-8538-4c4b-bcc9-9394c5e69e97 (impressions: 11th June 2023).

62 *Haaretz*, 11th May 2022, https://www.haaretz.com/israel-news/2022-05-11/ty-article/.premium/israeli-fathers-to-receive-paternity-leave-without-altering-partners-leave/00000180-d637-d452-a1fa-d7ff1eb50000 (impression: 12th June 2023).

63 UNICEF, https://www.unicef-irc.org/where-do-rich-countries-stand-on-childcare (impression: 12th June 2023).

64 Times of Israel, 20th August 2013, https://www.timesofisrael.com/reduced-child-allowance-benefits-come-into-effect/ (impression: 20th September 2023).

65 *Haaretz*, 9th March 2015, https://www.haaretz.com/science-and-health/2015-03-09/ty-article/ivf-in-israel-pros-and-cons/0000017f-da7b-d432-a77f-df7b83080000 (impression: 12th June 2023).

66 Dan Senor and Saul Singer, *The Genius of Israel: The Surprising Resilience of a Divided Nation in a Turbulent World*, London, Avid/Simon & Schuster, 2023, p. 105.

67 Ibid., p. 92.

68 Orna Donath, *Regretting Motherhood: A Study*, Berkeley, California, North Atlantic, 2017, pp. 6, 12.

69 Daily Citizen, 27th January 2023, https://dailycitizen.focusonthefamily.com/japanese-prime-minister-warns-of-imminent-societal-collapse-due-to-low-birth-rate/ (impression: 20th September 2023).

70 Deutsche Welle, 24th September 2005, https://www.dw.com/en/france-moves-to-encourage-large-families/a-1720921 (impression: 3rd July 2023).

71 Reuters, 17th January 2023, https://www.reuters.com/world/europe/france-sees-collapse-births-lowest-since-world-war-two-2024-01-16/ (impression: 25th January 2024).

72 R. Dinkel, 'Are the Pro-natalist Measures of the German Democratic Republic Succeeding? A Comparative Description of Fertility Trends in Both German States', *IFO Studies*, 30(2), 1984, pp. 139–62; *Daily*

Telegraph, 10th August 2000, https://www.telegraph.co.uk/news/worldnews/europe/germany/1352142/Germans-urged-to-have-more-babies.html (impressions: 7th July 2023).

73 *New York Times*, 27th October 2015, https://www.nytimes.com/2015/10/28/world/americas/in-cuba-an-abundance-of-love-but-a-lack-of-babies.html (impression: 3rd July 2023).

74 *Foreign Policy*, 23rd September 2016, https://foreignpolicy.com/2016/09/23/forget-one-child-beijing-wants-china-to-make-more-babies/ (impression: 20th July 2023).

75 *Guardian*, 18th May 2023, https://www.theguardian.com/politics/2023/may/18/miriam-cates-the-new-tory-darling-and-rising-star-of-the-right (impression: 7th July 2023).

76 Wikipedia, https://en.wikipedia.org/wiki/Miriam_Cates (impression: 7th July 2023).

5. How about Women?

1 Tax Foundation, 27th May 2021, https://taxfoundation.org/tax-relief-for-families-europe-2021/ (impression: 3rd July 2023).

2 HuffPost, 4th July 2022, https://www.huffingtonpost.co.uk/entry/sunday-times-article-tax-childless_uk_62c2a896e4b00a9334ea7083 (impression: 4th July 2023).

3 Shannon N. Wood et al., 'Need for and Use of Contraception by Women before and during COVID-19 in Four sub-Saharan African Geographies: Results from Population-based National or Regional Cohort Surveys', *Lancet Global Health*, 9, 2021, pp. e793–801.

4 Fauzia Akhter Huda et al., 'Contraceptive Practices among Married Women of Reproductive Age in Bangladesh: A Review of the Evidence', *Reproductive Health*, 14(1), 2017.

5 *Economist*, 18th February 2023, p. 25.

6 Eva Beaujouan and Caroline Berghammer, 'The Gap between Lifetime Fertility Intentions and Completed Fertility in Europe and the United States: A Cohort Approach', *Population Research and Policy Review*, 38, 2019, pp. 507–35.

7 Maryam Hosseini et al., 'The Gap between Desired and Expected

Fertility among Women in Iran: A Case Study of Tehran City', *PLOS One*, 16(9), 2021.

8   Wolfgang Lutz, 'The Future of Human Reproduction: Will Birth Rates Recover or Continue to Fall?', *Ageing Horizons*, 7, 2007, pp. 15–21.

9   Ohio State University, 12th January 2023, https://news.osu.edu/falling-birth-rate-not-due-to-less-desire-to-have-children/ (impression: 11th April 2023).

10 *Guardian*, 26th January 2020, https://www.theguardian.com/lifeandstyle/2020/jan/26/im-almost-50-and-full-of-regret-its-too-late-to-have-children-mariella-frostrup (impression: 6th September 2020).

11 Serap Kavas, 'The Gendered Division of Housework and Fertility Intention in Turkey', *Genus*, 75(21), 2019.

12 Anneli Miettinen et al., 'Women's housework decreases fertility: Evidence from a longitudinal study among Finnish couples', *Acta Sociologica*, 58(2), 2015, pp. 139–54.

13 Kaur Life, 20th April 2020, https://kaurlife.org/2020/04/20/silent-murders-female-infanticide-and-sex-selective-abortions-among-south-asians/ (impression: 7th July 2023).

14 *Independent*, 14th January 2014, https://www.independent.co.uk/news/science/the-lost-girls-it-seems-that-the-global-war-on-girls-has-arrived-in-britain-9059610.html (impression: 7th July 2023).

6. How about the Environment?

1   Peter Singer, *The Expanding Circle: Ethics and Sociobiology* [1981], Princeton, Princeton University Press, 2011.

2   *Washington Post*, 22nd December 2022, https://www.washingtonpost.com/climate-environment/2022/12/02/climate-kids/ (impression: 24th July 2023).

3   Pew Research Center, 19th November 2021, https://www.pewresearch.org/short-reads/2021/11/19/growing-share-of-childless-adults-in-u-s-dont-expect-to-ever-have-children/ (impression: 24th July 2023).

4   Elizabeth Marks et al., 'Young People's Voices on Climate Anxiety, Government Betrayal and Moral Injury: A Global Phenomenon', *Lancet Planet Health*, 5, 2021, pp. 863–73.

5 Macrotrends, https://www.macrotrends.net/countries/GBR/united-kingdom/infant-mortality-rate (impression: 24th July 2023). Note that the rate of infant mortality is the rate of death among those aged under one. The rate of those dying in childhood more generally has also fallen sharply.

6 UN Population Division, https://population.un.org/wpp2019/ (impression: 13th March 2023).

7 Our World in Data, https://ourworldindata.org/maternal-mortality (impression: 27th July 2023).

8 Ibid.

9 Our World in Data, https://ourworldindata.org/calorie-supply-sources (impression: 24th July 2023).

10 Ohio State University, April 2023, https://origins.osu.edu/read/hunger-not-eradicated-food-crisis-africa?language_content_entity=en (impression: 24th January 2024).

11 Our World in Data, https://ourworldindata.org/hunger-and-undernourishment (impression: 24th January 2024).

12 Our World in Data, https://ourworldindata.org/war-and-peace (impression: 24th July 2023).

13 Our World in Data, https://ourworldindata.org/natural-disasters (impression: 24th July 2023).

14 *Jewish Chronicle*, 21st July 2023, https://www.thejc.com/news/news/just-stop-oil-spokeswoman-claims-all-humans-are-in-a-giant-gas-chamber-4wvhav2B3A9OPTX7lVqolX (impression: 24th July 2023).

15 Richard Fuller et al., 'Pollution and Health: A Progress Update', *Lancet*, 6(6), 2022, pp. 535–47.

16 ONS, https://www.ons.gov.uk/aboutus/transparencyandgovernance/freedomofinformationfoi/ukdeathsrelatingtoexposuretopollution orpoorairquality (impression: 23rd July 2023).

17 *Guardian*, 16th December 2020, https://www.theguardian.com/environment/2020/dec/16/girls-death-contributed-to-by-air-pollution-coroner-rules-in-landmark-case (impression: 23rd July 2023).

18 Our World in Data, https://ourworldindata.org/water-access (impression: 24th July 2023).

19 UN Population Division, op. cit.

20 World Economic Forum, 12th September 2022, https://www.
weforum.org/agenda/2022/09/reading-writing-global-literacy-rate-
changed/ (impression: 23rd July 2023).

21 Our World in Data, https://ourworldindata.org/tertiary-education
(impression: 23rd July 2023).

22 NASA, https://climate.nasa.gov/global-warming-vs-climate-
change/ (impression: 24th July 2023).

23 M. L. Parry et al., 'Effects of Climate Change on Global Food
Production under SRES Emissions and Socio-economic Scenarios',
Global Environmental Change, 14(1), 2004, pp. 53–67.

24 Josef Schmidhuber and Francesco N. Tubiello, 'Global Food Security
under Climate Change', *PNAS*, 104(50), 11th December 2007, pp.
19703–8.

25 Food and Agriculture Organization of the United Nations,
'Agricultural Production Statistics 2000–2020: Analytical Brief
41', p. 3, https://www.fao.org/3/cb9180en/cb9180en.pdf.

26 Paul Morland, *Tomorrow's People: The Future of Humanity in Ten
Numbers*, London, Picador, 2022, p. 241.

27 Our World in Data, https://ourworldindata.org/grapher/arable-
land-pin (impression: 29th August 2023).

28 *Guardian*, 17th September 2012, https://www.theguardian.com/
environment/2012/sep/17/arctic-collapse-sea-ice (impression: 24th
July 2023).

29 *Guardian*, 6th June 2023, https://www.theguardian.com/
environment/2023/jun/06/too-late-now-to-save-arctic-summer-
ice-climate-scientists-find (impression: 24th July 2023).

30 European Space Agency, 13th May 2020, https://climate.esa.int/
en/projects/sea-ice/news-and-events/news/simulations-suggest-ice-
free-arctic-summers-2050/ (impression: 24th July 2023).

31 NSIDC, https://nsidc.org/arcticseaicenews/ (impression: 24th July
2023).

32 EOS, 11th February 2022, https://eos.org/science-updates/
new-perspectives-on-the-enigma-of-expanding-antarctic-sea-ice;
NOAA, 14th March 2023, https://www.climate.gov/news-features/
understanding-climate/understanding-climate-antarctic-sea-ice-
extent (impressions: 24th July 2023).

33 NOAA, 28th June 2023, https://www.climate.gov/news-features/event-tracker/antarctic-sea-ice-reaches-early-winter-record-low-june-2023 (impression: 24th July 2023).

34 Al Jazeera, 1st July 2014, http://america.aljazeera.com/articles/2014/7/1/kiribati-climatechange.html (impression: 24th July 2023).

35 ABC News [Australia], 7th January 2021, https://www.abc.net.au/news/2021-01-08/why-are-hundreds-of-pacific-islands-getting-bigger/13038430 (impression: 24th July 2023).

36 Qi Zhao et al., 'Global, Regional, and National Burden of Mortality Associated with Non-optimal Ambient Temperatures from 2000 to 2019: A Three-stage Modelling Study', *Lancet Planetary Health*, 5(7), July 2021, pp. e415–e425.

37 World Bank, https://data.worldbank.org/indicator/EN.ATM.CO2E.PC?name_desc=false (impression: 24th July 2023).

38 *Economist*, 19th August 2023, p. 61.

39 UK Department for Energy Security and Net Zero, https://assets.publishing.service.gov.uk/government/uploads/system/uploads/attachment_data/file/1168116/2021-local-authority-ghg-emissions-stats-summary-update-060723.pdf (impression: 24th July 2023).

40 ONS, https://www.ons.gov.uk/economy/nationalaccounts/uksectoraccounts/compendium/economicreview/october2019/thedecouplingofeconomicgrowthfromcarbonemissionsukevidence (impression: 24th July 2023).

41 Energy.gov, https://www.energy.gov/energysaver/furnaces-and-boilers (impression: 26th July 2023).

42 Macrotrends, https://www.macrotrends.net/countries/USA/united-states/carbon-co2-emissions (impression: 2nd August 2023).

43 Green Car Congress, 30th September 2019, https://www.greencarcongress.com/2019/09/20190930-sivak.html (impression: 26th July 2023).

44 Car and Driver, 28th February 2023, https://www.caranddriver.com/features/g15382442/best-gas-mileage-nonhybrid-cars-gasoline-nonelectric/ (impression: 26th July 2023).

45 *Daily Telegraph*, citing S&P Global Commodity Insights, 1st August 2023 https://www.telegraph.co.uk/business/2023/08/01/

china-clean-tech-revolution-leader-defeatist-britain/ (impression: 2nd August 2023).

46 World Economic Forum, 4th November 2021, https://www. weforum.org/agenda/2021/11/renewable-energy-cost-fallen/ (impression: 23rd July 2023).

47 IRENA, https://www.irena.org/Energy-Transition/Technology/ Energy-storage-costs (impression: 23rd July 2023).

48 Statista, https://www.statista.com/statistics/236657/global-crude-oil-reserves-since-1990/ (impression: 26th July 2023).

49 W. Stanley Jevons, *The Coal Question: An Enquiry concerning the Progress of the Nation and the Probable Exhaustion of our Coal Mines*, London and Cambridge, Macmillan, 1865.

50 *Scientist*, 28th October 2022, https://www.the-scientist.com/news-opinion/younger-scientists-are-more-innovative-study-finds-70700 (impression: 13th November 2023).

51 *Harvard Business Review*, January 2017, https://hbr.org/2017/01/ what-a-study-of-33-countries-found-about-aging-populations-and-innovation (impression: 6th February 2024).

52 Carnegie Endowment, 18th March 2010, https://carnegieendowment. org/2010/03/18/japan-s-past-and-u.s.-future-pub-40356 (impression: 26th July 2023).

53 Lee Branstetter and Yoshiaki Nakamura, 'Is Japan's Innovative Capacity in Decline?', in Magnus Blomström et al., eds, *Structural Impediments to Growth in Japan*, Chicago, Chicago University Press and National Bureau of Economic Research, 2003, pp. 195, 198.

54 Kazuo Nishimura, Dai Miyamoto and Tadashi Yagi, 'Japan's R&D Capabilities Have Been Decimated by Reduced Class Hours for Science and Math Subjects', *Humanities and Social Science Communications*, 9(210), 2022.

55 *MIT Technology Review*, 9th January 2023, https://www. technologyreview.com/2023/01/09/1065135/japan-automating-eldercare-robots/; *Neue Zürcher Zeitung*, 23rd November 2022, https:// www.nzz.ch/english/how-japan-is-using-technology-to-care-for-its-aging-population-ld.1713444 (impressions: 26th July 2023).

56 World Bank, https://data.worldbank.org/indicator/EN.ATM. CO2E.PC?name_desc=false (impression: 26th July 2023).

7. How about Immigration?

1   *Observer*, 6th August 2023, https://www.theguardian.com/commentisfree/2023/aug/06/conservative-calls-women-more-babies-hide-pernicious-motives (impression: 7th August 2023).

2   *The Voice*, 29th December 2022, https://www.voice-online.co.uk/news/uk-news/2022/12/29/will-the-caribbean-community-survive-population-decline/; ONS, https://www.ons.gov.uk/peoplepopulationandcommunity/culturalidentity/ethnicity/bulletins/ethnicgroupenglandandwales/census2021 (impressions: 27th July 2023).

3   Sylvie Dubuc, 'Fertility and Population in the UK: Trends and Outlooks', paper presented at the Population Association of America conference, 2009.

4   AP, 29th June 2020, https://apnews.com/article/ap-top-news-international-news-weekend-reads-china-health-269b3de1af34e17c1941a514f78d764c (impression: 28th July 2023).

5   Amnesty International, June 2006, https://www.amnesty.org/en/wp-content/uploads/2021/08/mde180042006en.pdf (impression: 28th July 2023).

6   Paul Morland, *The Human Tide: How Population Shaped the Modern World*, London, John Murray, 2019, p. 88.

7   Leslie King, 'Demographic Trends, Pronatalism and Nationalist Ideologies in the Late Twentieth Century', *Ethnic and Racial Studies*, 25(3), 2002, pp. 367–89.

8   See, for example, *Le Monde*, 9th March 2023, https://www.lemonde.fr/en/opinion/article/2023/01/09/presenting-the-pension-reform-as-fair-to-women-is-a-lot-of-hogwash_6010887_23.html (impression: 16th March 2024).

9   Paul Morland, *Tomorrow's People: The Future of Humanity in Ten Numbers*, London, Picador, 2022, p. 88.

10 Michelle J. K. Osterman et al., 'Births: Final Data for 2021', *National Vital Statistics Report*, 72(1), 2023, p. 26, https://www.cdc.gov/nchs/data/nvsr/nvsr72/nvsr72-01.pdf; India Budget, https://www.indiabudget.gov.in/economicsurvey/doc/stat/tab818.pdf (impressions: 28th July 2023).

11   UN Department of Economic and Social Affairs, 2021, https://www.un.org/development/desa/pd/sites/www.un.org.development.desa.pd/files/undesa_pd_2021_wpp-fertility_policies.pdf (impression: 15th March 2024).

12   UK Parliament, https://www.parliament.uk/about/living-heritage/transformingsociety/private-lives/yourcountry/overview/nationalservice/ (impression: 3rd August 2023).

13   Based on the difference between those aged 20–25 and those aged 6–65, as per UN Population Division, https://population.un.org/wpp2019/ (impression: 13th March 2023).

14   *Washington Post*, 7th January 2022, https://www.washingtonpost.com/politics/2022/01/07/economy-is-feeling-effects-fading-baby-boom/ (impression: 27th July 2023).

15   ONS, https://www.ons.gov.uk/employmentandlabourmarket/peoplenotinwork/unemployment/timeseries/mgsx/lms (impression: 27th July 2023).

16   ONS, https://www.ons.gov.uk/peoplepopulationandcommunity/populationandmigration/internationalmigration/articles/explore50yearsofinternationalmigrationtoandfromtheuk/2016-12-01 (impression: 27th July 2023).

17   Friedrich-Ebert-Stiftung, 2011, https://library.fes.de/pdf-files/id/ipa/08041.pdf (impression: 27th July 2023).

18   CountryEconomy.com, https://countryeconomy.com/countries/compare/poland/uk?sc=XEAB (impression: 27th July 2023).

19   World Bank, https://data.worldbank.org/indicator/NY.GDP.PCAP.PP.CD?locations=PL; World Bank, https://data.worldbank.org/indicator/NY.GDP.PCAP.PP.CD?locations=GB (impression: 15th March 2024).

20   The Migration Observatory, 2nd August 2022, https://migrationobservatory.ox.ac.uk/resources/briefings/migrants-in-the-uk-an-overview/ (impression: 27th July 2023).

21   Central Statistics Office Ireland, https://www.cso.ie/en/releasesandpublications/ep/p-pme/populationandmigrationestimatesapril2022/keyfindings/ (impression: 27th July 2023).

22   Dudley Kirk, *Europe's Population in the Interwar Years*, Princeton, League of Nations Publications, 1946, pp. 282–3.

23 Government of Luxembourg, https://luxembourg.public.lu/en/society-and-culture/international-openness/luxembourg-portugal.html (impression: 27th July 2023).

24 Full Fact, 13th February 2017, https://fullfact.org/europe/eu-has-shrunk-percentage-world-economy/ (impression: 27th July 2023).

25 *Cosmopolitan*, 19th December 2014, https://www.cosmopolitan.com/lifestyle/news/a34405/im-latina-and-i-dont-want-kids/ (impression: 2nd August 2023).

26 UN Population Division, op. cit.

27 Pew Research Center, 9th July 2021, https://www.pewresearch.org/short-reads/2021/07/09/before-covid-19-more-mexicans-came-to-the-u-s-than-left-for-mexico-for-the-first-time-in-years/ (impression: 23rd July 2023).

28 Darrell Bricker and John Ibbison, *Empty Planet: The Shock of Global Population Decline*, New York, Crown, 2019, p. 121.

29 Calculation based on data of UN Population Division, op. cit.

30 World Bank, https://data.worldbank.org/indicator/NY.GDP.PCAP.CD (impression: 15th March 2024).

31 Eric Kaufmann, *Whiteshift: Populism, Immigration and the Future of White Majorities*, London, Allen Lane, 2018, pp. 201–4.

32 European Principle Group, 24th April 2022, https://europeanprincipalgroup.com/insight/analysis-2nd-round-of-the-french-presidential-election-apr-24th/; CNN, 6th May 2022, http://edition.cnn.com/2002/WORLD/europe/05/05/france.win/ (impressions: 3rd August 2023).

33 Euronews, 30th June 2023, https://www.euronews.com/my-europe/2023/06/30/eu-summit-ends-with-a-whimper-as-poland-and-hungary-resist-migration-reform (impression: 3rd August 2023).

34 Gi-Wook Shin, 'Racist South Korea? Diverse but Not Tolerant', in Rotem Kowner and Walter Demel, eds, *Race and Racism in Modern East Asia*, Leiden and Boston, Brill, 2013, p. 369.

35 In My Korea, 26th December 2023, https://inmykorea.com/how-many-foreigners-in-korea/ (impression: 3rd August 2023).

36 Amnesty International, 10th March 2023, https://www.amnesty.org/en/latest/news/2023/03/tunisia-presidents-racist-speech-incites-a-wave-of-violence-against-black-africans/ (impression: 3rd August 2023).

37 Africa News, 15th July 2023, https://www.africanews.com/2023/07/15/tunisia-not-a-land-of-transit-or-settlement-president// (impression: 3rd August 2023).

38 UK Parliament, https://lordslibrary.parliament.uk/ugandan-asians-50-years-since-their-expulsion-from-uganda/ (impression: 3rd August 2023).

39 *Mail and Guardian* [South Africa], https://atavist.mg.co.za/ghana-must-go-the-ugly-history-of-africas-most-famous-bag/ (impression: 3rd August 2023).

40 Department of Health and Social Care, https://www.gov.uk/government/publications/code-of-practice-for-the-international-recruitment-of-health-and-social-care-personnel/code-of-practice-for-the-international-recruitment-of-health-and-social-care-personnel-in-england (impression: 4th August 2023).

41 *The Voice*, 30th March 2023, https://www.voice-online.co.uk/news/exclusive-news/2023/03/30/more-ghanaian-nurses-in-nhs-than-in-ghana/ (impression: 3rd August 2023).

8. What Technology Can Do for Us

1 F. K. Donnelly, 'Luddites Past and Present', *Labour*, 18, 1986, pp. 217–21.

2 Marxist Internet Archive, https://www.marxists.org/archive/marx/works/1848/communist-manifesto/ch01.htm (impression: 10th August 2023).

3 Energy Intelligence, 14th October 2022, https://www.energyintel.com/00000183-d5b7-da97-ad9f-d7f7e4e70000 (impression: 10th August 2023).

4 Statista, https://www.statista.com/statistics/281998/employment-figures-in-the-united-kingdom-uk/; 1911 Census, https://www.1911census.org.uk/1811 (impressions: 10th August 2023). Note that the 1811 census data are for Great Britain, whereas the workforce data include Northern Ireland as well.

5 John Maynard Keynes, *Essays in Persuasion*, New York, Harcourt Brace, 1932, pp. 358–73.

6 Our World in Data, https://ourworldindata.org/working-hours (impression: 10th August 2023).

7 Martin Ford, *The Rise of the Robots: Technology and the Threat of Mass Unemployment*, London, Oneworld, 2015, p. 32.

8 M. W. Linn, R. Sandifer and S. Stein, 'Effects of Unemployment on Mental and Physical Health', *American Journal of Public Health*, 75(5), 1985, pp. 502–6.

9 Our World in Data, https://ourworldindata.org/employment-in-agriculture (impression: 10th August 2023).

10 Statista, https://www.statista.com/topics/6880/food-trade-in-france/#topicOverview (impression: 10th August 2023).

11 Federal Reserve of St Louis, https://fred.stlouisfed.org/series/DEUPEFANA (impression: 10th August 2023).

12 Paul Morland, *Tomorrow's People: The Future of Humanity in Ten Numbers*, London, Picador, 2022, p. 67.

13 Gov.uk, https://www.gov.uk/government/statistics/taxi-and-private-hire-vehicle-statistics-england-2022/taxi-and-private-hire-vehicle-statistics-england-2022 (impression: 10th August 2023).

14 CompTIA, March 2023, https://www.cyberstates.org/pdf/CompTIA_State_of_the_tech_workforce_2023.pdf (impression: 10th August 2023).

15 PwC, https://www.pwc.co.uk/services/economics/insights/the-impact-of-automation-on-jobs.html (impression: 12th September 2023).

16 National Institute of Social and Economic Research, *Productivity in the UK: Evidence Review*, June 2022, p. 10, https://www.niesr.ac.uk/wp-content/uploads/2022/06/Productivity-in-the-UK-Evidence-Review.pdf?ver=VIgU5hfsI5mFdzSLFHvj.

17 OECD, https://stats.oecd.org/Index.aspx?DataSetCode=PDYGTH (impression: 17th March 2024).

18 Trading Economics, https://tradingeconomics.com/united-states/productivity (impression: 14th August 2023).

19 Brookings, 1st March 1999, https://www.brookings.edu/articles/the-solow-productivity-paradox-what-do-computers-do-to-productivity/ (impression: 14th August 2023).

20 Ford, 2015, op. cit.

21 Ibid., p. xii.

22 Ibid., pp. 122–3.

23 Ibid., pp. 161–5.

24 *MIT Technology Review*, 9th January 2023, https://www. technologyreview.com/2023/01/09/1065135/japan-automating-eldercare-robots/ (impression: 14th August 2023).

25 Ford, 2015, op. cit., pp. 177–8.

26 The Conversation, 23rd March 2023, https://theconversation.com/ we-were-told-wed-be-riding-in-self-driving-cars-by-now-what-happened-to-the-promised-revolution-201088 (impression: 14th August 2023).

27 Euronews, 20th September 2022, https://www.euronews.com/next/ 2022/09/20/will-self-driving-cars-on-our-roads-ever-be-a-reality-some-experts-are-becoming-sceptical (impression: 14th August 2023).

28 *Economist*, 2nd September 2023, p. 61.

29 Christopher Mims, *Arriving Today: From Factory to Front Door – Why Everything Has Changed about How and What We Buy*, New York, Harper Business, 2021, p. 142.

30 Martin Ford, *Rule of the Robots: How Artificial Intelligence Will Transform Everything*, London, Basic Books, 2021.

31 Jobst Landgrebe and Barry Smith, *Why Machines Will Never Rule the World: Artificial Intelligence without Fear*, Abingdon, Routledge, 2022. Carl Benedikt Frey and Michael Osborne, 'Generative AI and the Future of Work', Oxford Martin School Working Papers on the Future of Work, Oxford, Oxford Martin School, 2023, https://www. oxfordmartin.ox.ac.uk/downloads/academic/2023-FoW-Working-Paper-Generative-AI-and-the-Future-of-Work-A-Reappraisal-combined.pdf.

32 BBC, 3rd November 2023, https://www.bbc.co.uk/news/ uk-67302048 (impression: 1st December 2023).

9. What Government Can Do for Us

1 Tom Clark and Andrew Dilnot, 'Long-term Trends in British Taxation and Spending', IFS Briefing Notes, 25, Institute of Fiscal Studies, p. 2, https://ifs.org.uk/sites/default/files/output_url_files/

bn25.pdf; Statista, https://www.statista.com/statistics/298478/
public-sector-expenditure-as-share-of-gdp-united-kingdom-uk/
(impression: 23rd August 2023).

2   IMF, https://www.imf.org/external/datamapper/exp@FPP/USA/
FRA/JPN/GBR/SWE/ESP/ITA/ZAF/IND (impression: 22nd
August 2023).

3   Dubravka Šuica, speaking in Vienna, 28th April 2023. See European
Commission, 28th April 2023, https://ec.europa.eu/commission/
presscorner/detail/en/speech_23_2509.

4   Kathleen Dalton, *Theodore Roosevelt: A Strenuous Life*, New York,
Vintage, 2022, pp. 305–6.

5   Richard Nixon, 'President Nixon on Problems of Population Growth',
Population and Development Review, 32(4), 2006, pp. 771–82.

6   Paul Morland, *The Human Tide: How Population Shaped the Modern
World*, London, John Murray, 2019, pp. 41–99.

7   Marie-Monique Huss, 'Pronatalism in the Inter-war Period in
France', *Journal of Contemporary History*, 25(1), 1990, pp. 39–68.

8   Morland, 2019, op. cit., p. 100; Lauren E. Forcucci, 'Battle for Births:
The Fascist Pronatalist Campaign in Italy 1925 to 1938', *Journal of
the Society for the Anthropology of Europe*, 10(1), 2010, p. 1; David L.
Hoffmann, 'Mothers in the Motherland: Stalinist Pronatalism in Its
Pan-European Context', *Journal of Social History*, 34(1), pp. 35–54.

9   Leslie King, 'France Needs Children: Pronatalism, Nationalism, and
Women's Equity', *Sociological Quarterly*, 39(1), 1998, p. 44.

10 Revue Benefits, https://revenuebenefits.org.uk/child-benefit/policy/
where_it_all_started/ (impression: 22nd August 2023).

11 Tomáš Sobotka, Anna Matysiak and Zusanna Brzozwska, 'Policy
Responses to Low Fertility: How Effective Are They?', UNFPA,
2019, p. 23.

12 UN Department of Economic and Social Affairs, 2021, https://www.
un.org/development/desa/pd/sites/www.un.org.development.desa.
pd/files/undesa_pd_2021_wpp-fertility_policies.pdf (impression:
22nd August 2023).

13 The Budapest Beacon, 29th July 2014, https://budapestbeacon.com/
full-text-of-viktor-orbans-speech-at-baile-tusnad-tusnadfurdo-of-
26-july-2014/ (impression: 23rd August 2023).

14 Reuters, 28th July 2022, https://www.reuters.com/world/europe/hungarys-orban-says-his-anti-immigration-stance-not-rooted-racism-after-backlash-2022-07-28/ (impression: 23rd August, 2023).

15 Conservative Home, 14th February 2023, https://conservativehome.com/2023/02/14/demographic-collapse-and-what-we-can-learn-about-natalism-from-hungary-and-poland/ (impression: 24th August 2023).

16 András Klinger, 'Fertility and Family Planning in Hungary', *Studies in Family Planning*, 8(7), 1977, pp. 166–7.

17 UN Department of Economic and Social Affairs, op. cit.

18 Éva Berde and Áron Drabancz, 'The Propensity to Have Children in Hungary, with Some Examples from Other European Countries', *Frontiers in Sociology*, 7, 2022.

19 World Directory of Minorities and Indigenous People, https://minorityrights.org/country/hungary/ (impression: 23rd August 2023); Laura Szabó et al., 'Fertility of Roma Minorities in Central and Eastern Europe', *Comparative Population Studies*, 46, October 2021.

20 European Commission, https://commission.europa.eu/strategy-and-policy/policies/justice-and-fundamental-rights/combatting-discrimination/roma-eu/roma-equality-inclusion-and-participation-eu-country/hungary_en (impression: 24th August 2023).

21 Reporting Democracy, 23rd September 2021, https://balkaninsight.com/2021/09/23/helping-hungarians-have-all-the-babies-they-want/ (impression: 23rd August 2023).

22 Linda J. Cook et al., 'Trying to Reverse Demographic Decline: Pro-natalist and Family Policies in Russia, Poland and Hungary', *Social Policy and Society*, 22(2), 2022, pp. 355–75.

23 UN Department of Economic and Social Affairs, op. cit.

24 *European Conservative*, 27th October 2023, https://europeanconservative.com/articles/news/hungary-boosts-family-support-to-raise-birth-rate/ (impression: 1st December 2023).

25 *Guardian*, 4th March 2020, https://www.theguardian.com/world/2020/mar/04/baby-bonuses-fit-the-nationalist-agenda-but-do-they-work (impression: 23rd August 2023).

26 Ibid.

27 Eurostat, https://ec.europa.eu/eurostat/statistics-explained/index.php?title=Government_expenditure_on_defence (impression: 23rd August 2023).

28 Berde and Drabancz, op. cit.

29 Institute for Family Studies, 10th July 2018, https://ifstudies.org/blog/is-hungary-experiencing-a-policy-induced-baby-boom (impression: 23rd August 2023).

30 BNE Intellinews, 30th January 2023, https://www.intellinews.com/hungary-s-demographic-slide-continues-in-2022-268210/ (impression: 17th March 2024).

31 Statista, https://www.statista.com/statistics/1199245/hungary-women-of-childbearing-age-by-marital-status/ (impression: 23rd August 2023).

32 Hungary Today, 19th May 2022, https://hungarytoday.hu/number-of-marriages-eu-highest-number-hungary-european-union-weddings/ (impression: 23rd August 2023).

33 Cook et al., op. cit.

34 Australian Museum, 9th December 2021, https://australian.museum/learn/science/human-evolution/the-spread-of-people-to-australia/ (impression: 23rd August 2023).

35 Morland, 2019, op. cit., p. 13.

36 UN Department of Economic and Social Affairs, op. cit.

37 Treasury [Australia], 6th May 2002, https://treasury.gov.au/publication/2002-igr (impression: 20th March 2024).

38 *Sydney Morning Herald*, 3rd July 2022, https://www.smh.com.au/national/the-baby-bonus-generation-is-starting-to-turn-18-has-it-saved-australia-s-population-20220624-p5awfg.html (impression: 25th August 2023).

39 Ibid.

40 *Sydney Morning Herald*, 3rd May 2008, https://www.smh.com.au/national/rudd-to-end-baby-bonus-for-rich-20080503-gdsc1z.html (impression: 25th August 2023).

41 UN Department of Economic and Social Affairs, op. cit.

42 Robert Drago et al., 'Did Australia's Baby Bonus Increase the Fertility Rate?', *Population Research and Policy Review*, 30(3), p. 24.

43 *Financial Review*, 1st September 2017, https://www.afr.com/politics/
peter-costellos-baby-bonus-generation-grows-up-20170831-gy7wfg
(impression: 25th August 2023).

44 Treasury [Australia], 24th August 2023, https://ministers.treasury.
gov.au/ministers/jim-chalmers-2022/transcripts/national-press-
club-address-qa (impression: 20th March 2023).

45 Australian Institute of Family Studies, April 2023, https://aifs.gov.
au/research/facts-and-figures/births-australia-2023 (impression:
17th March 2024).

46 See, for example, Mei Fong, *One Child: The Story of China's Most
Radical Experiment*, London, Oneworld, 2016.

47 World Bank, https://data.worldbank.org/indicator/SP.DYN.TFRT.
IN?locations=CN (impression: 17th March 2024).

48 BBC, 17th January 2024, https://www.bbc.co.uk/news/world-asia-
china-68002803 (impression: 25th January 2024).

49 *Economist*, 21st January 2023, pp. 51–2.

50 Tian Wang and Quanbao Jiang, 'Recent Trend and Correlates of
Induced Abortion in China: Evidence from the 2017 China Fertility
Survey', *BMC Women's Health*, 22(1), 2022, p. 469; Statista, https://
www.statista.com/statistics/250650/number-of-births-in-china/
(impressions: 30th August 2023).

51 *Guardian*, 17th August 2022, https://www.theguardian.com/
world/2022/aug/17/chinese-government-birth-rate-policies-
abortions-population; *South China Morning Post*, 29th July 2022,
https://www.scmp.com/tech/policy/article/3186924/year-after-
chinas-private-tutoring-crackdown-classes-have-moved (impressions: 29th August 2023).

52 *Economist*, 29th September 2022, https://www.economist.com/
china/2022/09/29/china-is-trying-to-get-people-to-have-more-
babies (impression: 29th August 2023).

53 *Economist*, 21st January 2023, op. cit.

54 UN Expert Group Meeting on Policy Responses to Low Fertility,
2nd–3rd November 2015, https://www.un.org/development/desa/pd/
sites/www.un.org.development.desa.pd/files/undp_egm_201511_
policy_brief_no._4.pdf; *Inroads*, 2018, https://inroadsjournal.ca/
quebecs-childcare-program-20-2/; Statistics Canada, https://

www150.statcan.gc.ca/n1/pub/71-607-x/71-607-x2022003-eng.
htm (impressions: 12th September 2023).
55 Sobotka, Matysiak and Brzozwska, op. cit.

56 IMF, 22nd July 2022 https://www.imf.org/en/Publications/fandd/
issues/Series/Analytical-Series/new-economics-of-fertility-doepke-
hannusch-kindermann-tertilt (impression: 30th August 2023).

57 Re mental health, see Mental Health Foundation, https://www.
mentalhealth.org.uk/explore-mental-health/statistics/relationships-
community-statistics. Re law and order, see Stacey Bosick and Paula
Fomby, 'Family Instability in Childhood and Criminal Offending
during the Transition into Adulthood', *American Behavioural
Scientists*, 62(11), 2018, pp. 1483–504. Re emissions, see Buildings
and Cities, 9th February 2021, https://www.buildingsandcities.
org/insights/commentaries/sustainability-single-households.html
(impressions: 10th September 2023).

58 Cook et al., op. cit.

10. What We Can Do for Ourselves

1 Institute for Family Studies, 11th October 2017, https://ifstudies.
org/blog/in-georgia-a-religiously-inspired-baby-boom (impression:
31st August 2023).

2 Note that much of the fall was caused by emigration, a great deal
of it to Russia, following the dissolution of the Soviet Union.

3 Carnegie Europe, 23rd July 2021, https://carnegieeurope.
eu/2021/07/23/orthodox-church-in-georgia-s-changing-society-
pub-85021 (impression: 17th March 2024).

4 *Economist*, 5th June 2014, https://www.economist.com/middle-
east-and-africa/2014/06/05/make-more-babies (impression: 1st
September 2023).

5 *Harper's Bazaar*, 1st August 2019 https://www.harpersbazaar.com/
uk/celebrities/news/a28574274/why-the-duke-and-duchess-of-
sussex-wont-have-more-than-two-children/ (impression: 16th April
2024).

6 British Social Attitudes, https://bsa.natcen.ac.uk/latest-report/

british-social-attitudes-30/personal-relationships/homosexuality. aspx (impression: 31st August 2023).

7   BBC, 26th March 2015, https://www.bbc.com/news/uk-32061822 (impression: 17th March 2024).

8   The unit has been spun off and now offers services to governments across the world.

9   NHS Organ Donation, 20th May 2021, https://www.organdonation. nhs.uk/get-involved/news/family-and-public-support-helping-save-lives-one-year-on-from-the-introduction-of-max-and-keira-s-law/ (impression: 24th January 2024).

10 ONS, https://www.ons.gov.uk/peoplepopulationandcommunity/ birthsdeathsandmarriages/conceptionandfertilityrates/bulletins/ conceptionstatistics/2021 (impression: 1st September 2023).

11 Gov.uk, https://www.gov.uk/government/collections/teenage-pregnancy (impression:17th March 2024).

12 ABC News [US], 25th April 2018, https://abcnews.go.com/Health/ number-pre-teen-moms-us-record-low-cdc/story?id=54720089 (impression: 1st September 2023).

13 Kai Part et al., 'Teenage Pregnancies in the European Union in the Context of Legislation and Youth Sexual and Reproductive Health Services', *AOGS*, 92(12), 2013, pp. 1395–406.

14 *Varsity*, 15th October 2021, https://www.varsity.co.uk/news/22211 (impression: 17th March 2024).

15 Forbes, 4th June 2020, https://www.forbes.com/sites/ davidhessekiel/2020/06/04/companies-taking-a-public-stand-in-the-wake-of-george-floyds-death/?sh=5fd11111e7214; Lovin Dublin, 2nd June 2020, https://lovindublin.com/news/irish-businesses-showing-support-for-the-black-lives-matter-movement (impressions: 1st September 2023).

16 *Independent*, 3rd October 2014, https://www.independent.co.uk/ news/people/tracey-emin-there-are-good-artists-that-have-children-they-are-called-men-9771053.html (impression: 1st September 2023).

17 *Vogue*, 14th May 2023, https://www.vogue.co.uk/article/creativity-and-motherhood (impression: 4th September 2023).

18 See, for example, Qur'an 81:8.

19 Islam Question and Answer, https://islamqa.info/en/an`swers/13492/ does-islam-encourage-large-families (impression: 17th March 2024).

20 For an understanding of how nuanced the debate is even within Orthodox Judaism, see Lea Taragin-Zeller, *The State of Desire: Religion and Reproductive Politics in the Promised Land*, New York, New York University Press, 2023.

21 Population Reference Bureau, June 2002, https://www.prb.org/ wp-content/uploads/2016/09/IransFamPlanProg_Eng.pdf (impression: 11th April 2023).

22 Sriya Iyer, 'Religion and the Decision to Use Contraception in India', *Journal for the Scientific Study of Religion*, 41(4), 2002, pp. 711–22.

23 Jennifer Aengst, 'The Politics of Fertility: Politics and Pronatalism in Ladakh', *Himalaya*, 32(1), 2012.

24 World Bank, https://data.worldbank.org/indicator/SP.DYN.TFRT. IN; World Bank, https://data.worldbank.org/indicator/NY.GDP. PCAP.CD (impressions: 17th March 2024).

25 Pew Research Center, 21st September 2021, https://www. pewresearch.org/religion/2021/09/21/religious-composition-of-india/; Statista, https://www.statista.com/statistics/642137/malaysia-fertility-rates-by-ethnic-group/; *Colombo Telegraph*, 31st December 2019, https://www.colombotelegraph.com/index.php/facts-and-fallacies-of-muslim-population-in-sri-lanka/ (impressions: 11th April 2023).

26 BBC, 4th July 2023, https://www.bbc.co.uk/news/business-66030048 (impression: 12th September 2023).

27 Roberta Rutigliano and Mariona Lozano, 'Do I Want More If You Help Me? The Impact of Grandparental Involvement on Men's and Women's Fertility Intentions', *Genus*, 78(13), 2022.

28 Simon N. Chapman et al., 'Offspring Fertility and Grandchild Survival Enhanced by Maternal Grandmothers in Pre-industrial Society', *Scientific Reports*, 11(1), 2021.

ACKNOWLEDGEMENTS

I would like to thank my agent, Andrew Lownie, and my editor, Mark Richards, for helping me translate a concept into a book. Michelle Rosen-Oberman has once again been enormously helpful in preparing the text. I much appreciate the meticulous work of Alex Middleton and Alex Billington on the manuscript.

Many friends and family members have contributed to the thinking and writing that went into *No One Left*, both through conversation and through comments on the text. In particular I would like to thank Kevin Chang, Andress Goh, Daniel Hess, Nick Lowcock, Claire Morland, Sonia Morland, Philip Pilkington, Ian Price, Michael Wegier and Ed West. I continue to benefit from the encouragement and stimulation of David Goodhart and Eric Kaufmann. I greatly appreciate the time and thoughtfulness of Erika Bachiochi, Julia Chain, Mary Harrington and Louise Perry.

Although I am always grateful to my family for their inspiration and support, it is especially the case with this book since it is so intimately tied up with matters close to home: my mother Ingrid, my daughters Sonia and Juliet and their husbands Joel and Samuel, my son Adam and his fiancée Hannah, and above all my wife Claire and our grandsons, Leo and Hallel, to whom this book is dedicated.

INDEX

childcare costs 72
employment in 168
fertility rates 12, 28, 71
labour shortages 24
old-age dependency ratio 101
population 10, 44–5
pro-natal policy 116
working hours 166
Ghana 66, 158–9
global warming 132–7
government debt 21, 32, 35–7
government policies 52, 177–95
absence of 177–8
anti-natal 12, 90, 180
Australia 185–8
China 12, 116, 144, 145, 179–80
Cuba 116
France 115, 178–9, 180
Germany 116
Hungary 181–5
Latvia 180
on population density 82–3
pro-natal 82, 99–100, 115–17,
178–91
history of 178–80
impacts of 183–5, 187–8, 191–2
political positioning of 145–6
UK 116–17, 177–8, 180
USA 178
government spending 34–5, 177
on pro-natal policies 183, 184
grandparents 110, 209–10
Greece 58, 104
gross domestic product see GDP
growth
economic 26, 31–2, 84–5, 91–2
see also population growth
Guardian, The (newspaper) 116, 122
Guatemala 153
Guinea 47

Haredi Jews 40, 101, 207
Harry, Duke of Sussex 200
healthcare systems and infrastructure 14, 46, 109, 158–9
Herzl, Theodor 97
Hinduism 64, 89–90, 94, 206, 207
Hitler, Adolf 179
Holocaust 97, 98–9, 105
home ownership 73, 183, 194
homogeneity
cultural 156–7
ethnic 31–2, 181
hope 132
housework 78, 123, 192, 210
housing 60, 208–9
costs of 73, 194
government financial support
for 183, 194
HuffPost (news website) 119
humanity
potential loss of 42, 125–7, 134–5,
211–12
as resource 137–41
Hungary 145, 156, 181–5, 191
hyper-natalism 52

Ibbison, John 153
Ilia II, Patriarch of the Georgian
Orthodox Church 196–8
illiteracy 131
immigrants
education and skills of 24, 155,
158–9, 160
fertility rates of 65, 143, 151
retirement of 147
immigration 7, 57–8, 107–8, 143–61,
185
as biological imperialism 157–9,
161
costs of 160–1

United States of America (*cont.*)
  government debt 37
  government policies,
    pro-natal 178
  and immigration 155
  old-age dependency ratio 21
  population age 34
  productivity 171
  working hours 166
urbanisation
  development of 46, 82, 90, 164
  and fertility rates 48–9, 77, 96
  population density 17

Villepin, Dominique de 115

wages 19, 25, 33
war 44–5, 97
  deaths from 130
  and fertility rates 106–9, 127–8
water, access to 131
wealth 16, 77, 111
  fertility rates, impact on 71–2,
    193–4
welfare benefits *see* benefits, child;
    benefits, parental
welfare state 34–5
West Bank 109
Wilders, Geert 156
William, Prince of Wales 199
women 24–5, 119–24
  childbirth, reduced risks of 129
  childless, proportions of 59
  education of 66–8, 193, 210
    in Africa 48, 52–3
    in Indonesia 88
    in Israel 103
    and marriage 77, 103
  fertility, control of 88

fertility, desired 55–6, 68–9, 87–8,
    121–2
  pro-natal pressure on 111
  proportion of, in population 77,
    123–4
  rights of 58, 120–3, 192, 210
  in workforce 186, 192, 210
work *see* labour
workforce
  age group ratios in 20, 189
  age of entry to 19
  demand for 164–5, 166–7, 168–9
  labour, changes in 169–70
  older people in 6, 19, 147
  and population age 14
  population decline 8
  and robotics 172–3
  service sector 168–9, 170
  tech sector 169, 170
  technological impact on 162–4
  younger people 85
workforce shortages 6–7, 24–6
  in care sector 8–9
  due to retirement 154
  historical 146–7
  and markets 33
  in medicine and healthcare 158–9
  and old-age dependency
    ratio 19–22, 189–90
working-age population 26
World Economic Forum 136

younger people
  anti-natalism,
    environment-related 127
  fertility rates of 29
  innovation by 22–3, 138–40
  proportion of, in population 80–1
  in workforce 85

www.ingramcontent.com/pod-product-compliance
Lightning Source LLC
Chambersburg PA
CBHW020528270326
41927CB00006B/489